Windows System and User Tools

by

Dr Alfonso J. Kinglow

ISBN: 978-0-359-19948-8

Library of Congress Control Number: 2018911914

Printed in The United States of
America

DEDICATION

To my wife, Sarah for her Love and dedication,
And my daughters Sarah, Keren and Karina
My Strength, my Light and my Joy; and my five
Grandchildren
You have made me a proud Father,
Grandfather and a better man. I Love you all.

Some Items and Tables are available on the Internet and/or in the Public Domain. They have been Compiled and Tabulated for clarity and ease of use to find the subject, and to benefit all users and readers.

When necessary and possible; the Source is provided to encourage the users and readers to seek and search for additional information on the subject.

PREFACE

After my last classes, where I taught Basic, Intermediate and Advance Windows hardware and software, I wanted to put all the relevant information from my other books into one complete Book that would include Windows versions that were popular, like Windows 7, 8, 8.1 and 10. if I could consolidate and put all the information and graphics I was teaching, into one Book, it would be great. This Book would benefit all users and beginners, with all the information and tools that are available to them in Windows, but some Tools in Windows are hidden., and should be made available to everyone. And I have made those Tools available to the users in this book.

In this book I present all the System and User Tools that are available, to empower the users from beginners to advanced, so that they will have the Tools they should have, and know how to use them, so that they would not be taken advantage of, like they have been; from large companies exploiting the Seniors and beginners, just because they do not know anything about their hardware or Windows Operating Systems. Enough is Enough.

Understanding how to use the basic Tools is essential to becoming a Standard and
Professional User, and one day a Super-User. We now have Holographic Software been used with Windows 10 and new WiFi Standards that will more than double the speeds of Wi-Fi that we have now. These new Standards will change the way we work and use Computers. New Technologies that are been developed will make us more productive and give us Tools that we did not have before.

Understanding the various versions of Windows that you have will be significant in understanding how Windows work and its capabilities. Having the correct version of Windows will be important for the user to know; as it will affect the Software that users may want to run on their machines.

This book have some of the special Graphics I developed to better explain how Windows work in certain environments and what to expect.

I also present information on Free Tools and Utilities that will clean the Registry and System, and enhance the Performance and Security of the machine.

I also introduce several hidden Tools and Utilities to correctly Shutdown Windows, these Tools were built- in Windows, but hidden from the users.

After reviewing many computer books over the years, I discovered that they all assume that the reader's have some basic knowledge of computers and that they understand the entire Computer lingo's that are used. All of their assumptions are wrong, and lead sometimes to misconceptions. This new Book takes into account Windows 7, 8, 8.1 and 10 and all of the new Software and Utilities now available to users that were not available during the first publication of my first book in 2014.

Since then, Technologies have changed and new Technologies are now available to the users to allow them to monitor and troubleshoot their own hardware and software. New hidden Utilities and hidden Codes in Windows 10 are presented to empower users to explore and investigate. New and Free Software and Utilities are available on the Internet, where to go and get them is presented in this new Consolidated Book, " The All Windows Computer Book."

Almost all of the computer books I reviewed did not have, or did not include any basic Computer Terms or Acronyms used, or did not explain the meaning of some basic Computer Concepts that all users should know.

This book assumes nothing, and tries to present basic computer information in a plain and simple format, which includes some hidden features and commands that all users should know about; but are not published. These hidden features are basic information built into the hardware and Windows Software, but are not considered important enough by Windows designers, for the readers and users to know about.

This book gives the user a complete knowledge of computer Hardware and Software and current related Standard's up to date.

An emphasis is placed on current and new Wi-Fi standards that applies to new Technology today, and why they are important. I review the Wireless Standards (**802.11 b/g/n)** and the Standards **802.11/a/b/AC and AD** and the newest Standard 802.11/a/b/**AX.** That will be available in in 2019.

CONTENTS

SOFTWARE PROPERTIES AND ORGANIZATION.__ A Graphic View.

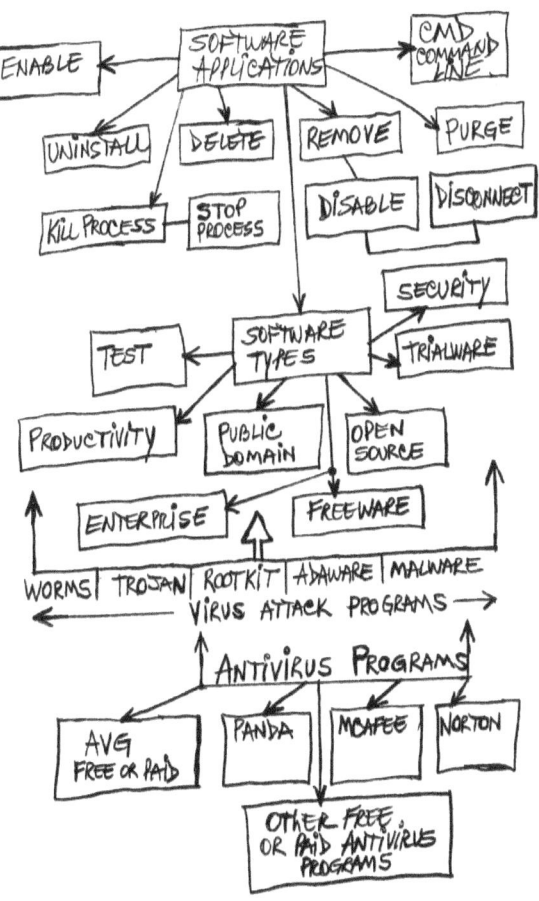

CHAPTER ONE

BASIC COMPUTER SPECS FOR A NEW COMPUTER.

Desktop or Laptop.

Windows Operating System (OS) recommended:

Windows 10 Professional – 64 Bit Operating System

Processor: INTEL Dual Core – i-5, i-7, or i-9

AMD Processors, are not recommended.

Installed RAM Memory: 8GB DDR3 minimum. Do not buy Computers with 3 GB. of Memory; or 6GB of Memory. (Memory Standards are 1, 2, 4, 8, 16, 32, 64, 128 GB. Etc.. (3 GB and 6 GB does not conform to the Memory Standard.)

Storage Hard Drive C:> must be at least 1 TB. (One Terabyte) or more...

Network Card: Must be 802.11 AC (the New

Standard) for Wi-Fi. And for Wired Network:
Gigabit Ethernet Card. Do not buy Computers
with

802.11 a/b/g or n Card, for Wi Fi Networks, as its
outdated and very slow.

Graphic Card: NVIDIA or ATI HD
Graphics or better

Video Display Screen: 15.4 Inches or 17 inch Wide.
Twenty Inch or higher Monitor, for use
with Desktop Towers.

Hardware Brands: LENOVO, HP,
SAMSUNG, SONY, TOSHIBA, ACER,
DELL, etc..

Computers are Sold at: Walmart, Best
Buy, Staples, Office Max, Costco, etc..

Windows Basic Things to know.__

Windows many different versions are
available, and its very important to know

which version you have and which version
will be the best for you.

If you want the latest version, then that will
be Windows 10, older versions will be
Windows 7, 8, 8.1 and Vista
Much older versions will be Windows XP,

Windows Vista, etc.. that are no longer
supported. In addition to the version, you
will need to know the kind of OS
(Operating System) either 64 Bit or 32 Bit.
A faster machine and very up to date will be
the 64 Bit OS.

Depending on what type of Software you
will be using on the Windows machine, you
must select the correct version.
A Graphic Chart is presented to Help you
decide. It is recommended that you
select the Professional version of
Windows, to get the maximum support
and Performance.

WINDOWS EDITIONS AND VERSIONS.—

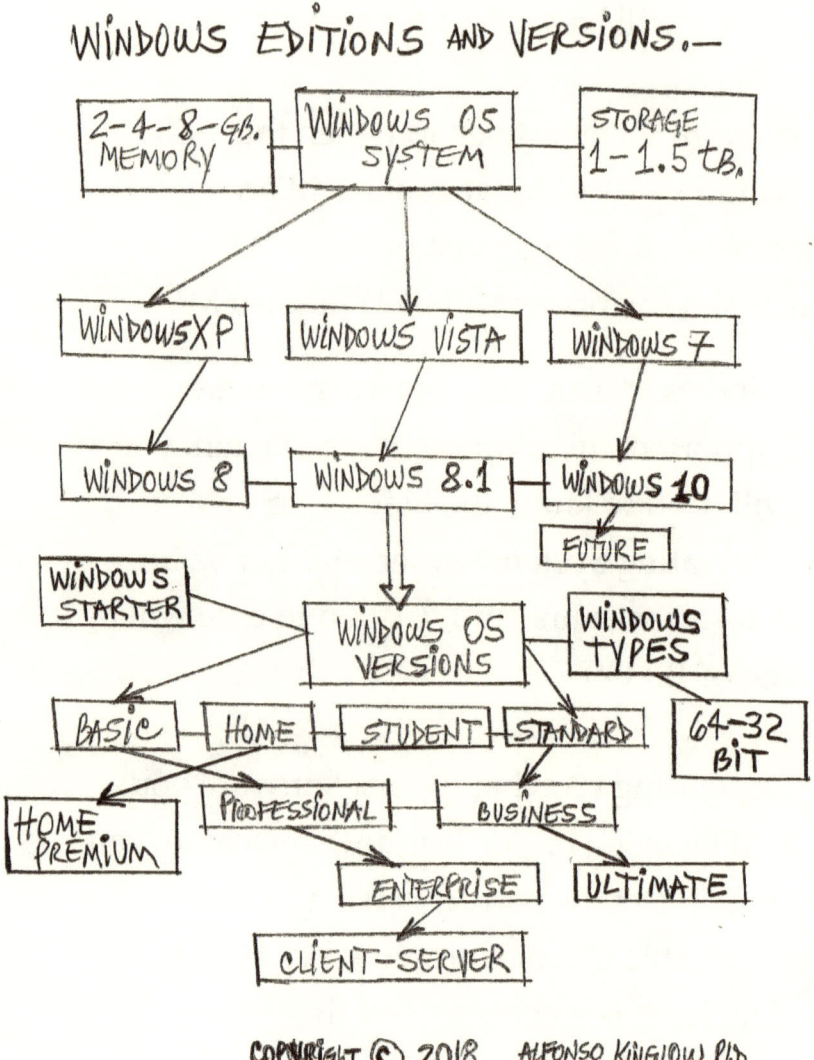

How to get more Performance from
Windows.__

Go to the RUN Command window, or go to Cortana on the lower left side of the screen with a Circle. Click on the Circle or inside the RUN
Command window, and type the following:
sysdm.cpl

A window is displayed, Select the Advanced Tab.
And go to Performance, select Settings.
In Settings; Select " Adjust for best Performance", click Apply, then OK or just Exit.

You have now setup the Windows Computer for Best Performance.

System Properties   ✕

| Computer Name | Hardware | Advanced | System Protection | Remote |

Windows uses the following information to identify your computer on the network.

Computer description: [AL COMPUTER]

For example: "Kitchen Computer" or "Mary's Computer".

Full computer name: Alfonso-PC

Workgroup: WORKGROUP

To use a wizard to join a domain or workgroup, click Network ID.   [Network ID...]

To rename this computer or change its domain or workgroup, click Change.   [Change...]

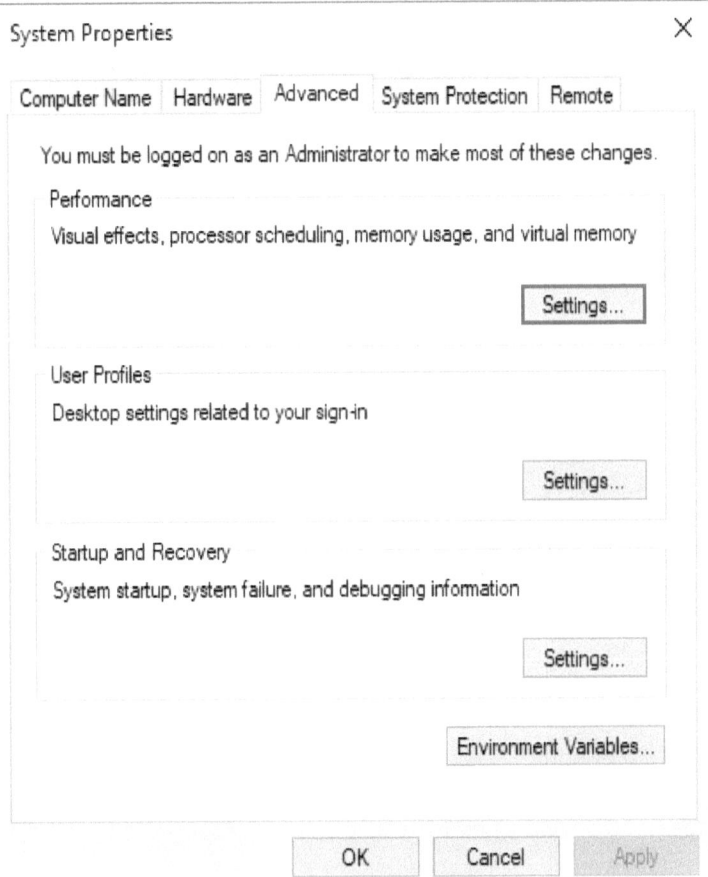

Visual Effects | Advanced | Data Execution Prevention

Select the settings you want to use for the appearance and performance of Windows on this computer.

○ Let Windows choose what's best for my computer

○ Adjust for best appearance

○ Adjust for best performance

● Custom:

- ☑ Animate controls and elements inside windows
- ☐ Animate windows when minimizing and maximizing
- ☐ Animations in the taskbar
- ☑ Enable Peek
- ☑ Fade or slide menus into view
- ☑ Fade or slide ToolTips into view
- ☑ Fade out menu items after clicking
- ☐ Save taskbar thumbnail previews
- ☐ Show shadows under mouse pointer
- ☑ Show shadows under windows
- ☑ Show thumbnails instead of icons
- ☐ Show translucent selection rectangle
- ☐ Show window contents while dragging
- ☑ Slide open combo boxes
- ☑ Smooth edges of screen fonts
- ☑ Smooth-scroll list boxes
- ☑ Use drop shadows for icon labels on the desktop

| OK | Cancel | Apply |

How to Shutdown Windows 10 with the built-in Utility.

There are many ways to correctly " Shutdown" Windows 10 Computers. The Standard way from the Start Menu and the CONTROL + ALT+ DEL , using the Control, the Alt Key and Delete Key at the same time to get to TASK MANAGER, and Shutdown the Computer.

There is another way. Using the built-in utility (Control Panel Item) called: slide to shutdown.exe

The Utility is located in C:/windows/system32 folder on the Hard drive.

Copy the Utility: slide to shutdown.exe to the Desktop so it can be available, when you are ready to shutdown.

The Control Panel .__

The heart of Windows is the Control Panel. Control Panel Items can be copied to the Desktop so they can be available immediately when they are needed.

The most Important Control Panels are:

1. Administrative Tools
2. Control Panel
3. Device Manager
4. Network and Sharing Center
5. Power Options
6. Programs and Features
7. Recovery

8. Security and Maintenance

9. System Information

10. System

11. Troubleshooting

12. User Accounts

13. Windows Defender Firewall

14. Work Folders

Windows User Tools.___

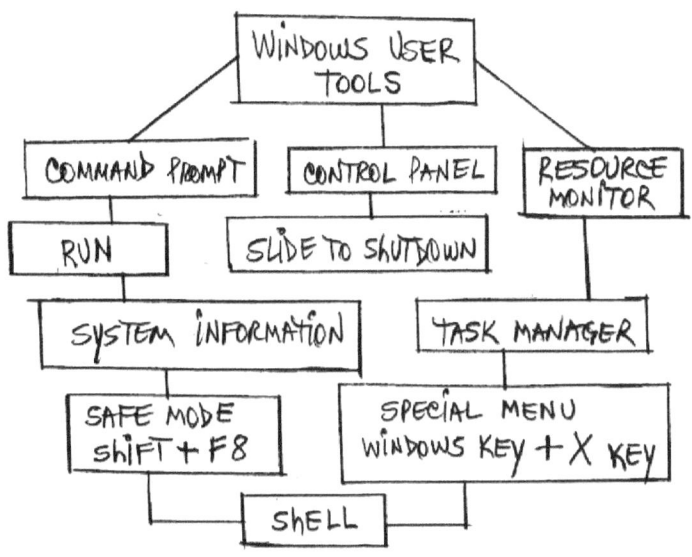

The most important Tools the User have access to in Windows are: The Command Prompt, The Control Panel, the RUN command, Resource Monitor, Shell, the Task Manager, Slide to Shutdown and the System Information.

Create the Special Advance Folder.__

The Special Advanced folder is the most important Folder that will ever be created. This folder contains over 200 files that are Tabulated and Organized to
Help the User Resolve any and all problems with Windows.

When the Folder is created it will be different from any Windows Folder. It will be Green or Blue, with symbols.

Follow the instructions to Create this Folder, which is Recommended for all Users.

CREATE A NEW FOLDER, CALL IT: ADVANCED.

Put a Period. After the **D.**

ENTER THE CODE AFTER YOU OPEN BRACKET, CLOSE BRACKET AT THE END.

OPEN BRACKET{

CLOSE BRACKET}

Advanced.{ED7BA470-8E54-465E-825C-99712043E01C}

<ENTER>

Software.__

Software are the Programs that make all of the Hardware work. The major software in any computer system will be the OS or Operating System such as Windows. The other major software will be the Applications and Utilities. Some software will need to be installed by the user and some will be installed by the OS or Operating System. Major user software will be the Applications such as Microsoft Office, and others that will facilitate the users to become more productive. Utilities will protect the computer from threats and viruses.

Software programs in general are divided into the following areas: Software Applications, Productivity, Games, Development, Multimedia, Educational, Utilities, System, LAN Local Area Networks, Web Software, Maintenance, Network, Paint, Accessories, Programming, Basic, Communications, Cloud Software, WAN Wide Area Network (The Internet), Graphics, Antivirus, etc...

Software programs are Installed, Deleted, Removed, and Purged.

When a Software program is Installed, it must be Un-Installed.

When a software program is Deleted, it must be Un-Deleted.

To correctly remove Software Programs, it must be done in the Control Panel in Programs and Features, if you are running Windows 8. The program is then Uninstalled or Changed.

Dragging a program to the Trash or

Recycle Bin does not Remove it, to
Remove a program it must be Shredded in
the Recycle Bin.

To Destroy a program it must be Purged.

Most Software are in the following modes,
Virtual Software, Hyper-V Software, Free
Software, Search Software, Shared Software,
Open Source Software, Public Domain
Software,
License Software, Encrypted Software,
Decrypted Software, Cipher Software,
Network
Card Test Software or (loop back address
Software), OS Windows Software(Operating
Systems); Firewall Software, Security
Software(
Bit Locker), Printer Software, Email
Software, DSL Router Software, etc..

Software Languages and Standards. __

Most Software are written in the following computer languages: Hypertext, used in Web Browsers on the Internet, Unix, Basic, Ada, C and C++ (C Plus Plus), Html (Hypertext Markup Language), Xml   (Extensible Markup Language), Fortran, Pascal, and High Level Compilers, etc....

The Standards that govern Software are: Defacto Standards, IEEE Project 802.x, The OSI Model and the ISO (International Standards Organization).

The Seven Pillars to Execute Software Programs.__

1. Setup and Install the Software

2. Uninstall and Undelete

3. Add and Remove

4. User Install and System Install

5. Run, Search and Delete

6. Free, Trial and Test

7. Open Source and Public Domain software access

Search Software Formats. __

The following Search Software Formats are used on the Internet as follows:

Search with --------©AND or + --- ©
---- Red Cars and Red Vans. Green Apples + Red Apples.

Search with -------© OR ----------© One word to
be in search (Flight Attendant

Stewardess.)

Search with ------®AND NOT (-) - ®
suv AND

NOT auto   (suv – auto)

Search with ----®   Phrase Searching --®
Exact

Phrase within   " Harry Potter"
                        Quotation.

Search with ----®   Wildcard ---® WRIT* CLOU* -®
The   Asterisk at the end of words.

Semantic Search Engines on the Internet.__

1. DuckDuckGo

2. Dogpile

3. WebCrawler

4. Ask.com

5. Hakia.com

6. Momma.com

Semantic Search and the Semantic Web.__

While *Semantic Web* and *Semantic Search* are
not the same thing, the two concepts are often
confused.

The fact that these two families of
technologies share the word *semantic*
has led to some confusion about the
difference between them. According
to MerriamWebster, semantic means
"of or related to meaning." Both of
these kinds of technologies attempt
to retrieve and present information
based on its meaning rather than on
its structure or intended usage, as
more traditional technologies do.

Although they are related, the two technologies in fact solve different problems.

In brief, Semantic Search is useful for searching on a single type of data in a single domain, whereas Semantic Web technologies are useful for querying across many types of related information. Consider a few examples of each kind of technology.

Although Google generally does a good job in ranking web pages, most of us know that this kind of search completely fails in other contexts. For example, searching your own computer for a document by relying on keywords can be very frustrating—not to mention searching a data store the size of your corporate intranet! In such cases, you will not succeed unless you know exactly what you are looking for. This shortfall is not the fault of the technology itself;

This is where Semantic Search comes in. Rather than blindly returning anything that contains the text you typed into the search bar, Semantic Search takes into account the *context* of your search as well as the underlying meaning of the documents to be searched.

However, what if you were searching for *jaguar*, the predatory black feline? Or *Jaguar*, the Mac 10.2 operating system? Or *Jaguar*, the Atari system? Even on Google, straightforward keyword searching <u>does not take into account the context of your search, nor does it understand the meaning of the documents.</u>

In an attempt to do a better job, Semantic Search technologies employ various methods

(NLP, statistical modeling, etc.), to categorize and/or cluster related documents to ease searching.

Semantic Web.____

The Semantic Web is a set of technologies for representing, storing, and querying information. Although these technologies *can* be used to store textual data—such as text in a Word document or PDF file—they typically are used to store smaller bits of data. Thus, while Semantic Search focuses largely on textual information, **the Semantic Web** also includes numbers, dates, figures, and other data in addition to text.

Semantic Web and Semantic Search Combined

Generally speaking, anything that can be accomplished with Semantic

Search can be represented as a Semantic Web query. That is, Semantic Web technologies are sufficiently broad to encompass all Semantic Search capabilities.

A simple way to think about which family of technologies might be useful for a specific problem is to ask yourself whether your users are searching on only one kind of information (e.g., restaurants, a flight number, etc.), or whether they are searching on many kinds of information (e.g., which presidents had children who did not live in the White House).

Semantic Web vendors focus on solving problems using many different kinds of information. Instead of simply storing data about restaurants, a Semantic Web application would have access to information about the chefs, the cities, the menus, the cuisine styles, the décor, the wine list, the wineries that produced the wine on the wine list, etc.

However, if you need to answer a question such as, "What restaurants in Boston have several wines that were produced in the Alsace region between 1998 and 2001?" then Semantic Search will not be able to help you; instead, you will need the Semantic Web.

Hardware.__

The Hardware is the box or frame that contains all the major parts of a computer, the internal hard drive, the CD/DVD Player, the different input ports, the keyboard and mouse, the processor and ram memory, the Ethernet network card, the Wireless network card, the video display, the LCD display(on laptops), the sound card, the internal built in camera, the internal microphone, etc.. One of the major Ports is the USB (Universal Serial Bus) that is now used to connect Printers, Cameras and multiple other devices to your computer hardware.

Policies are built into the computer hardware to allow for security and to manage the hardware.
Some of the most important policies are the SECPOL. MSC (Security Policy) and GPEDIT. MSC (Group Policy Editor) these policies allow you to setup the security configuration on your computer hardware. These policies are launched using the Command Line (CMD) built into your computer, or by typing the policy directly into the START or RUN line. The Command Line CMD is provided as a means of accessing your Computer Hardware and Software policies and to directly manage a great part of your computer hardware,

without requiring any software to manage policies.

It is used also for direct maintenance of the computer and comes with a reasonable help file. This file contains all of the commands used with the CMD. The command line window when launched appears with a black background. The background and text colors can be changed from a menu of different colors as well as the text size and window size. Some preferred combinations are; red background with yellow text color or green background with white or purple text color, etc... To change the color background and text, click on the CMD icon in the upper left side of the command window.

To access all of the standard policies to set up your computer hardware you can find them in the MMC (Microsoft Management Console) built into your computer hardware.

The MMC allow the user to create Snap-in's to setup the hardware and security configuration. To access the MMC just type it into the CMD window or directly into the START or RUN line, on the lower left side of your computer.

A View of Computer Configuration with Applications and Utilities. ____

The User Tools and System Tools are presented in a
Graphic configuration easy to understand. All the Diagnostic Tools that are built-into Windows are shown and are available to the user, for diagnostics and troubleshooting the computer.

Twelve Diagnostic Tools are shown that are built into Windows. All these tools can be access by the user. If the Computer is running Windows 10, just type in the name of the tool in Cortana, to access, or just type the name into the Start area for all other Systems.

MORE PERFORMANCE FROM WINDOWS OS.

To get more Performance from Windows OS, open the Taskbar and type: sysdm.cpl into the underline search box.

Next press <Enter>

Switch to the Advanced Tab, under the Performance, click the Settings button to disable Windows Animations, Fades, Font smoothing, drop shadows behind dialog boxes, and other visual enhancements that take up more memory and processor time.

To keep Windows as visually back as possible, click the "Adjust for Best Performance" Checkbox; Exit and Restart.

Setup Windows <u>Power Option</u> in the Control
Panel.

Goto the Control Panel in Windows, open the
Power Options App

Setup each of the Power Options like the
handouts, they must be set to Never, Never,
Never and Do
Nothing, example like" When I close the lid"; Do
Nothing..etc..

Windows Shortcuts. ___

SHIFT + F8 when Computer is Booting, To
Access " SAFE MODE" to fix Computer

Windows Key + X for Special MENU

Open RUN and Type in: Shell:AppsFolder To
Access the " All Applications" Folder

"Slide to Shutdown" Windows Utility, is located
in:
C:>/windows/system32 on the Hard Drive.

TO KEEP YOUR COMPUTER CLEAN AND ENHANCE PERFORMANCE AND ELIMINATE MALWARE, ADAWARE AND SPYWARE. ___

Download the following Utilities and RUN them at least Once a Week or every two weeks.

Advanced System Care 11

Glary Utility 5.100

Clean Master 6.0

Acebyte Utility 3.2

BASIC   INFORMATION   ABOUT   WINDOWS TOOLS.

Windows User Tools

8. Command prompt

9. Control Panel

10. Resource Monitor

11. Run Command

12. Slide to Shutdown

13. System Information

14. Task Manager

15. Safe Mode Shift + F8

16. Special Menu Windows Key + "X" Key

17. Shell

<u>Windows Diagnostic Tools:</u>

MSConfig from RUN

3D Builder

Narrator

Performance monitor

Resource Monitor

RUN Command

System Configuration

Task Manager

Windows System Tools:

1. On Screen Keyboard

2. Phone companion

3. Phone

4. System Information

5. Uninstall

6. Windows memory Diagnostic

7. Win Patrol Explorer

8. Win Patrol Help

9. CMD Command Line

Windows Administrative Tools

15. Computer Management

16. Defragment drives

17. Disk Cleanup

18. Event Viewer

19. ISCSI Initiator

20. Local Security Policy

21. ODBC Data Sources

22. Performance Monitor

23. Print Management

24. Recovery Drive

25.Resource Monitor

26.Services

27.System Configuration

28.System Information

29.Task Scheduler

30.Windows defender Firewall

31. Windows Memory Diagnostic

 Get more Performance from Windows with sysdm.cpl

   using RUN. Goto Settings in Performance tab.

NOTES

CHAPTER TWO

USING EXPLORER SHELL.

TO CREATE A PORTABLE FOLDER OF ANY
PART OF WINDOWS SYSTEM.__

USING " EXPLORER SHELL"

10. Create a Short Cut Folder by selecting
    NEW and Shortcut

11. In the Shortcut window: Type:
    Explorer Shell: and the name of the
    Part of Windows you want to create:
    for Example:

    Explorer
Shell:ControlPanelFolder   and click
NEXT   another window will be
displayed.

Type the name you want to give to the folder, and press <Finish>

The new Control Panel Folder will be created.

Another Example: Explorer Shell:AppsFolder The All Applications Folder will be Created.

1. This folder will be portable and can be used on any Windows Computer.

SOME WINDOWS SHELL COMMANDS.
____

You can use any of the following commands to create the desired shortcut:

explorer shell:MyComputerFolder (for My Computer   shortcut) explorer shell:RecycleBinFolder (for Recycle

Bin   shortcut) explorer
shell:ControlPanelFolder (for Control
Panel   shortcut) explorer
   shell:Administrative   Tools   (for
Administrative   Tools   shortcut)
explorer
shell:ChangeRemoveProgramsFolder (for
Programs and Features shortcut) explorer
   shell:NetworkPlacesFolder (for
Network   shortcut) explorer
shell:Favorites   (for   Favorites shortcut)
explorer   shell:HomegroupFolder   (for
<u>Homegroup</u>   shortcut) explorer
shell:Games (for Games shortcut)
explorer   shell:Fonts (for   Fonts
shortcut) explorer shell:UserProfiles
(for Users folder shortcut) explorer
shell:Profile (for your username
folder   shortcut) explorer
shell:Public   (for   Public
folder shortcut) explorer shell:My
Documents (for Documents
shortcut)
explorer   shell:Common   Documents   (for

Public   Documents   shortcut)
explorer shell:My Music (for Music folder
shortcut)
explorer   shell:CommonMusic   (for   Public
Music   folder   shortcut)   explorer   shell:My
Pictures (for Pictures folder shortcut)

explorer shell:CommonPictures (for Public
Pictures   folder   shortcut) explorer
shell:My Video (for Videos folder shortcut)
explorer   shell:CommonVideo   (for   Public
Videos   folder   shortcut)   explorer
shell:Downloads   (for   Downloads
folder   shortcut)   explorer
shell:CommonDownloads   (for
Public
Downloads   folder   shortcut)
explorer shell:::{3080F90E-D7AD-11D9-
BD980000947B0257} (for Flip 3D or Window
Switcher shortcut)

EXTENDED SHELL COMMANDS :

Shell Command   Description
shell:AccountPictures   Account Pictures
shell:AddNewProgramsFolder   The "Get
Programs" Control panel item
shell:Administrative Tools   Administrative
Tools shell:AppData   Same as
%appdata%, the
c:\user\<username>\appdata\roaming folder
shell:Application Shortcuts   Opens the folder
which stores all Modern apps shortcuts
shell:AppsFolder   The virtual
folder which stores all installed Modern apps
shell:AppUpdatesFolder   The "Installed
Updates" Control panel item
shell:Cache   IE's cache folder
(Temporary Internet Files) shell:CD Burning
Temporary Burn Folder
shell:ChangeRemoveProgramsFolder   The
"Uninstall a program" Control panel item
shell:Common Administrative Tools   The
Administrative Tools folder for all users
shell:Common AppData   The

C:\ProgramData folder (%ProgramData%)

shell:Common Desktop   Public Desktop shell:Common Documents Public Documents

shell:Common Programs   All Users Programs, which are part of Start menu. Still used by the Start screen

    shell:Common Start Menu   All Users Start Menu folder, same as above

    shell:Common Startup   The Startup folder, used for all users

    shell:Common Templates   Same as above, but used for new documents templates, e.g. by Microsoft Office

    shell:CommonDownloads   Public Downloads

    shell:CommonMusic   Public Music shell:CommonPictures Public Pictures shell:CommonRingtones Public Ringtones folder

    shell:CommonVideo   Public Videos shell:ConflictFolder   The Control Panel\All Control Panel Items\Sync Center\Conflicts item

shell:ConnectionsFolder   The
Control
Panel\All Control Panel Items\Network
Connections item
shell:Contacts   Contacts folder
(Address book) shell:ControlPanelFolder
Control Panel shell:Cookies
The folder with IE's cookies
shell:CredentialManager
C:\Users\<username>\AppData\Roaming\Micros
oft\Credentials
shell:CryptoKeys
C:\Users\<username>\AppData\Roaming\Micros
oft\Crypto
shell:CSCFolder   This folder is
broken in Windows 8/7, provides access to
the Offline files item
shell:Desktop   Desktop
shell:Device Metadata Store
C:\ProgramData\Microsoft\Windows\
DeviceMet adataStore
shell:DocumentsLibrary
Documents Library shell:Downloads
Downloads folder shell:DpapiKeys

C:\Users\<username>\AppData\Roaming\Micros
oft\Protect

shell:Favorites   Favorites

shell:Fonts

C:\Windows\Fonts shell:Games

The Games Explorer item

shell:GameTasks

shell:HomeGroupFolder   The Home Group
root folder

shell:ImplicitAppShoC:\Users\<username>\AppD
ata\Local\Microsoft\Windows\GameExplorer

  shell:History

  C:\Users\<username>\AppData\Local\Micro
  soft \Windows\History, IE's browsing history
  shell:HomeGroupCurrentUserFolder   The
  Home Group folder for the current user
  rtcuts

 C:\Users\<username>\AppData\Roaming\Micro
 s oft\Internet Explorer\Quick Launch\User
 Pinned\ImplicitAppShortcuts

  shell:InternetFolder   This shell
  command will start Internet Explorer
  shell:Libraries   Libraries
  shell:Links   The "Favorites"

folder from the Explorer navigation pane.

shell:Local AppData

C:\Users\<username>\AppData\Local

shell:LocalAppDataLow

C:\Users\<username>\AppData\LocalLow

shell:LocalizedResourcesDir   This shell folder is broken in Windows 8

shell:MAPIFolder   Represents the Microsoft Outlook folder shell:MusicLibrary Music Library shell:My Music   The "My Music" folder

(not the Library) shell:My Pictures

The "My Pictures" folder

(not the Library) shell:My Video

The "My Videos" folder

(not the Library)

shell:MyComputerFolder

Computer/Drives view

shell:NetHood

C:\Users\<username>\AppData\Roamin g\Micros   oft\Windows\Network Shortcuts   shell:NetworkPlacesFolder The Network Places folder which shows computers and devices on your network shell:OEM Links   This shell command does nothing on my Windows 8 Retail edition. Maybe it works with OEM Windows 8 editions. shell:Original Images   Not functional on Windows 8

shell:Personal   The "My Documents" folder (not the Library)

shell:PhotoAlbums   Saved slideshows, seems to have not been implemented yet

shell:PicturesLibrary   Pictures Library shell:Playlists   Stores WMP Playlists. shell:PrintersFolder The classic "Printers" folder (not 'Devices and Printers') shell:PrintHood C:\Users\<username>\AppData\Roaming\Micro s oft\Windows\Printer Shortcuts

shell:Profile   The User profile folder

shell:ProgramFiles   Program Files

shell:ProgramFilesCommon   C:\Program Files\Common Files

shell:ProgramFilesCommonX86 C:\Program Files (x86)\Common Files - for Windows x64 shell:ProgramFilesX86 C:\Program Files (x86) - for Windows x64

shell:Programs

C:\Users\<username>\AppData\Roamin g\Micros oft\Windows\Start Menu\Programs (Per-user Start Menu Programs folder)

shell:Public   C:\Users\Public

shell:PublicAccountPictures C:\Users\Public\AccountPictures

shell:PublicGameTasks C:\ProgramData\Microsoft\Windows\GameE xplo rer

shell:PublicLibraries C:\Users\Public\Libraries

shell:Quick Launch C:\Users\<username>\AppData\Roaming\Micros oft\Internet Explorer\Quick Launch

shell:Recent   The "Recent Items" folder (Recent Documents)

shell:RecordedTVLibrary The "Recorded TV" Library

shell:RecycleBinFolder Recycle Bin shell:ResourceDir

C:\Windows\Resources where visual styles are stored

shell:Ringtones
C:\Users\<username>\AppData\Local\Microsoft\Windows\Ringtones

shell:Roamed Tile Images   Is not implemented yet. Reserved for future.

shell:Roaming Tiles
C:\Users\<username>\AppData\Local\Microsoft\Windows\RoamingTiles

shell:SavedGames   Saved Games

shell:Screenshots   The folder for Win+Print Screen screenshots

shell:Searches   Saved Searches   shell:SearchHomeFolder Windows Search UI

shell:SendTo   The folder with items that you can see in the "Send to" menu

shell:Start Menu
C:\Users\<username>\AppData\Roaming\Micros oft\Windows\Start Menu (Per-user Start Menu folder) shell:Startup Per-user Startup folder

shell:SyncCenterFolder   Control

Panel\All Control Panel Items\Sync
Center

shell:SyncResultsFolder   Control
Panel\All Control Panel Items\Sync
Center\Sync Results shell:SyncSetupFolder
Control Panel\All Control Panel Items\Sync
Center\Sync Setup shell:System
C:\Windows\System32
shell:SystemCertificates
C:\Users\<username>\AppData\Roaming\Micr
os oft\SystemCertificates
shell:SystemX86
C:\Windows\SysWOW64 -Windows x64 only
shell:Templates
C:\Users\<username>\AppData\Roaming\Micros
oft\Windows\Templates
shell:User Pinned   Pinned items for
Taskbar and Start screen,
C:\Users\<username>\AppData\Roaming\Micros
oft\Internet Explorer\Quick Launch\User Pinned
shell:UserProfiles   C:\Users, the
users folder where the user profiles are
stored shell:UserProgramFiles   Not
implemented yet. Reserved for future.

shell:UserProgramFilesCommon

same as above shell:UsersFilesFolder

The current user profile

shell:UsersLibrariesFolder   Libraries

shell:VideosLibrary   Videos

Library shell:Windows

C:\Windows

shell:DpapiKeys

C:\Users\<username>\AppData\Roaming\Micros oft\Protect

shell:Favorites   Favorites

shell:Fonts

C:\Windows\Fonts   shell:Games

The   Games   Explorer   item shell:GameTasks

    C:\Users\<username>\AppData\Local\Microso ft

    \Windows\GameExplorer

    shell:History

    C:\Users\<username>\AppData\Local\Mic rosoft \Windows\History, IE's browsing history shell:HomeGroupCurrentUserFolder

    The Home Group folder for the current user

shell:HomeGroupFolder   The Home
Group root folder

shell:ImplicitAppShortcuts
C:\Users\<username>\AppData\Roaming\Micr
os oft\Internet Explorer\Quick Launch\User
Pinned\ImplicitAppShortcuts

shell:InternetFolder   This shell
command will start Internet Explorer

shell:Libraries   Libraries

shell:Links   The "Favorites"
folder from the Explorer navigation pane.

shell:Local AppData
C:\Users\<username>\AppData\Local

shell:LocalAppDataLow
C:\Users\<username>\AppData\LocalLow

shell:LocalizedResourcesDir   This shell folder
is broken in Windows 8

shell:MAPIFolder   Represents
the Microsoft Outlook folder

shell:MusicLibrary   Music
Library shell:My Music   The
"My Music" folder
(not the Library) shell:My Pictures
The "My Pictures" folder

(not the Library) shell:My Video
The "My Videos" folder
(not the Library)
shell:MyComputerFolder
Computer/Drives view
shell:NetHood
C:\Users\<username>\AppData\Roamin
g\Micros   oft\Windows\Network
Shortcuts   shell:NetworkPlacesFolder
The Network Places folder which shows
computers and devices on your network
shell:OEM Links   This shell
command does nothing on my Windows
8 Retail edition. Maybe it works with
OEM Windows 8 editions. shell:Original
Images   Not functional on
Windows 8

shell:Personal   The "My
Documents" folder (not the Library)
shell:PhotoAlbums   Saved
slideshows, seems to have not been
implemented yet
shell:PicturesLibrary   Pictures
Library shell:Playlists   Stores
WMP Playlists. shell:PrintersFolder

The classic "Printers" folder (not 'Devices and Printers') shell:PrintHood C:\Users\<username>\AppData\Roaming\Micros oft\Windows\Printer Shortcuts

shell:Profile   The User profile folder
shell:ProgramFiles   Program Files

shell:Programs C:\Users\<username>\AppData\Roaming\Micros oft\Windows\Start Menu\Programs (Per-user Start Menu Programs folder)

shell:Public   C:\Users\Public
shell:PublicAccountPictures C:\Users\Public\AccountPictures shell:PublicGameTasks C:\ProgramData\Microsoft\Windows\G ameExplo rer shell:PublicLibraries C:\Users\Public\Libraries

shell:Quick Launch C:\Users\<username>\AppData\Roaming\Micros oft\Internet Explorer\Quick Launch

shell:Recent   The "Recent Items" folder (Recent Documents)

shell:RecordedTVLibrary   The "Recorded TV" Library

shell:RecycleBinFolder   Recycle

Bin shell:ResourceDir

C:\Windows\Resources where visual styles

are stored

shell:Ringtones

C:\Users\<username>\AppData\Local\

Microsoft \Windows\Ringtones

shell:Roamed Tile Images   Is not

implemented yet. Reserved for future.

shell:Roaming Tiles

C:\Users\<username>\AppData\Local\Microsoft

\Windows\RoamingTiles

shell:SavedGames   Saved Games

shell:Screenshots   The folder for

Win+Print Screen screenshots

shell:Searches   Saved Searches

shell:SearchHomeFolder   Windows Search UI

shell:SendTo   The folder with

items that you can see in the "Send to" menu

shell:Start Menu

C:\Users\<username>\AppData\Roami

ng\Micros oft\Windows\Start Menu

(Per-user Start Menu folder) shell:Startup

Per-user Startup folder

shell:SyncCenterFolder   Control

Panel\All Control Panel Items\Sync
Center

shell:SyncResultsFolder   Control
Panel\All Control Panel Items\Sync
Center\Sync Results shell:SyncSetupFolder
Control Panel\All Control Panel Items\Sync
Center\Sync Setup shell:System
C:\Windows\System32

shell:SystemCertificates
C:\Users\<username>\AppData\Roaming\Micr
os oft\SystemCertificates

shell:SystemX86
C:\Windows\SysWOW64 -Windows x64 only

shell:Templates
C:\Users\<username>\AppData\Roaming\Micr
os oft\Windows\Templates

shell:User Pinned   Pinned items for
Taskbar and Start screen,
C:\Users\<username>\AppData\Roaming\Micros
oft\Internet Explorer\Quick Launch\User Pinned

shell:UserProfiles   C:\Users, the
users folder where the user profiles are
stored shell:UserProgramFiles   Not
implemented yet. Reserved for future.

shell:UserProgramFilesCommon

same as above shell:UsersFilesFolder

The current user profile

shell:UsersLibrariesFolder   Libraries

shell:VideosLibrary   Videos

Library shell:Windows

C:\Windows

How Windows 10 is Organized
on the
Desktop.__

Several Graphics are presented to explain how Windows 10 is organized.

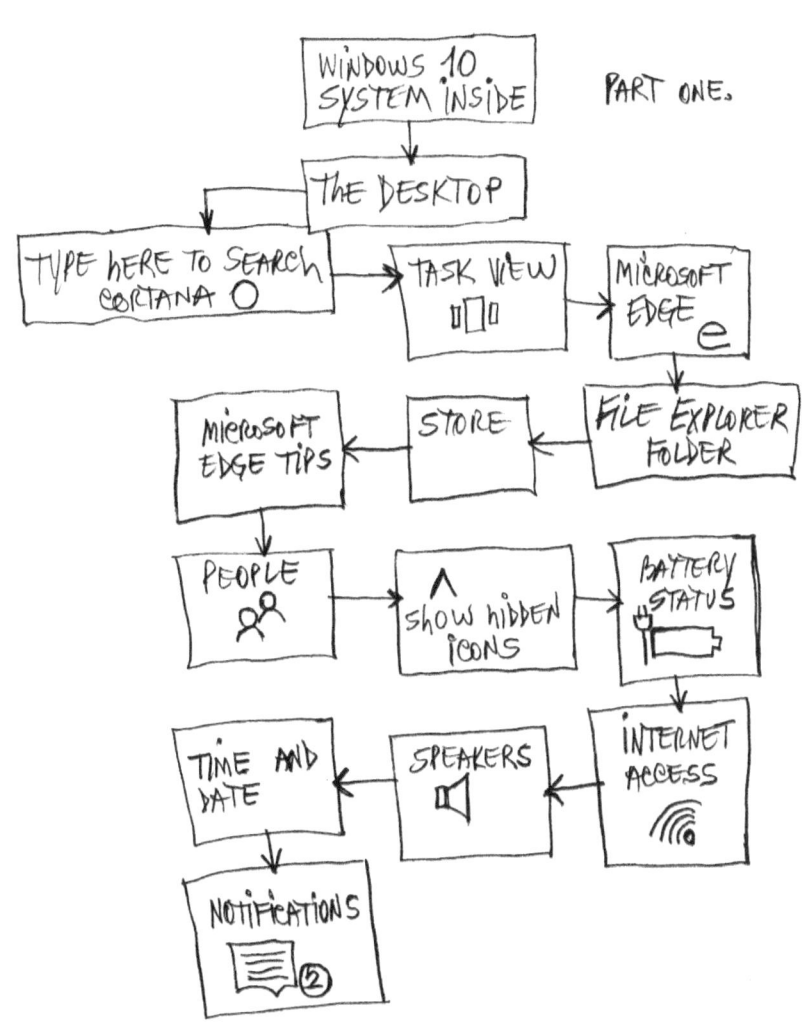

PART ONE.

2018 COPYRIGHT ©ALFONSO J. KINGLOW

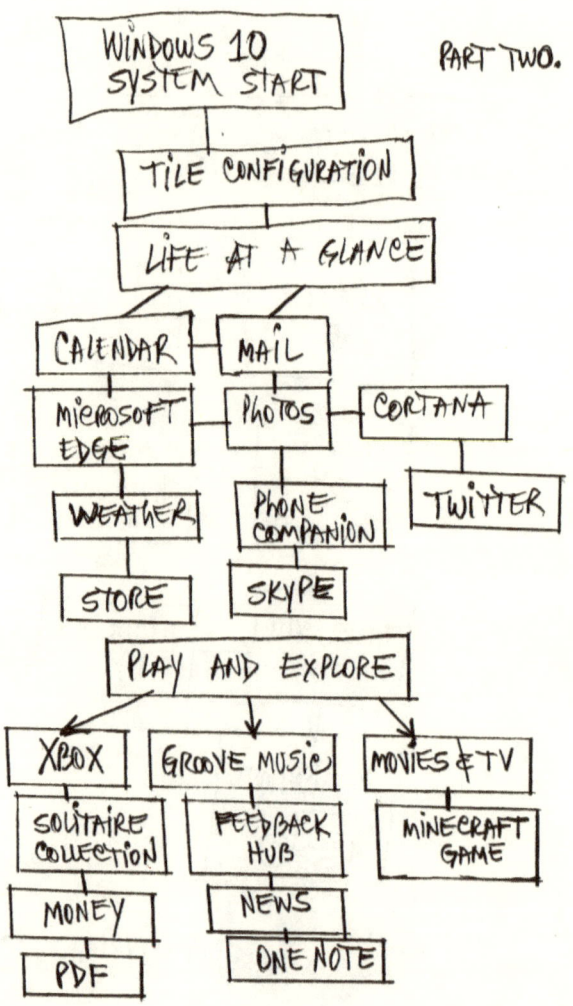

PART TWO.

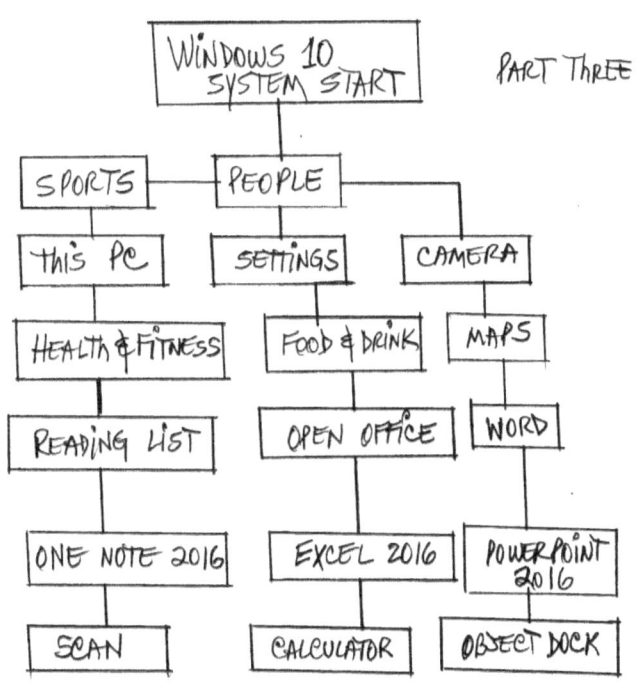

WINDOWS 10 SYSTEM START

PART THREE

SPORTS — PEOPLE

THIS PC — SETTINGS — CAMERA

HEALTH & FITNESS — FOOD & DRINK — MAPS

READING LIST — OPEN OFFICE — WORD

ONE NOTE 2016 — EXCEL 2016 — POWERPOINT 2016

SCAN — CALCULATOR — OBJECT DOCK

2018 COPYRIGHT © ALFONSO J. KINGLOW

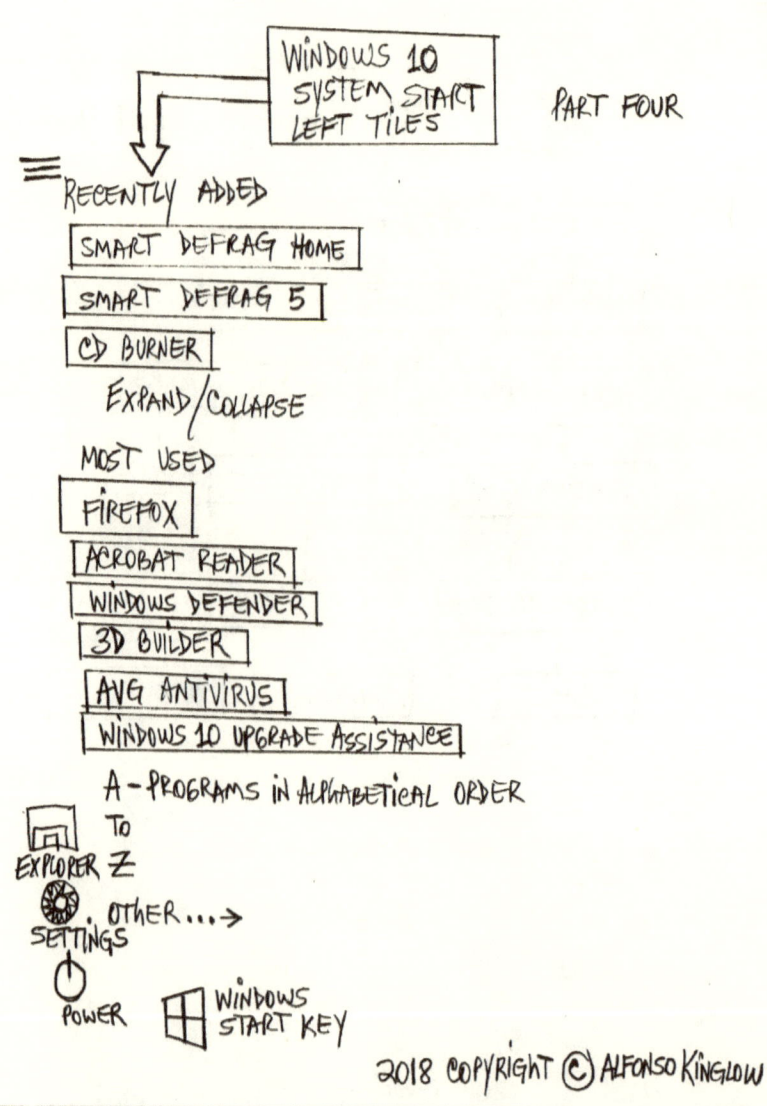

WINDOWS 10
SYSTEM START
LEFT TILES

PART FOUR

RECENTLY ADDED

SMART DEFRAG HOME

SMART DEFRAG 5

CD BURNER

EXPAND/COLLAPSE

MOST USED

FIREFOX

ACROBAT READER

WINDOWS DEFENDER

3D BUILDER

AVG ANTIVIRUS

WINDOWS 10 UPGRADE ASSISTANCE

A - PROGRAMS IN ALPHABETICAL ORDER
TO
EXPLORER Z

OTHER...→
SETTINGS

POWER   WINDOWS
         START KEY

The Complete Windows 10 Layout.__

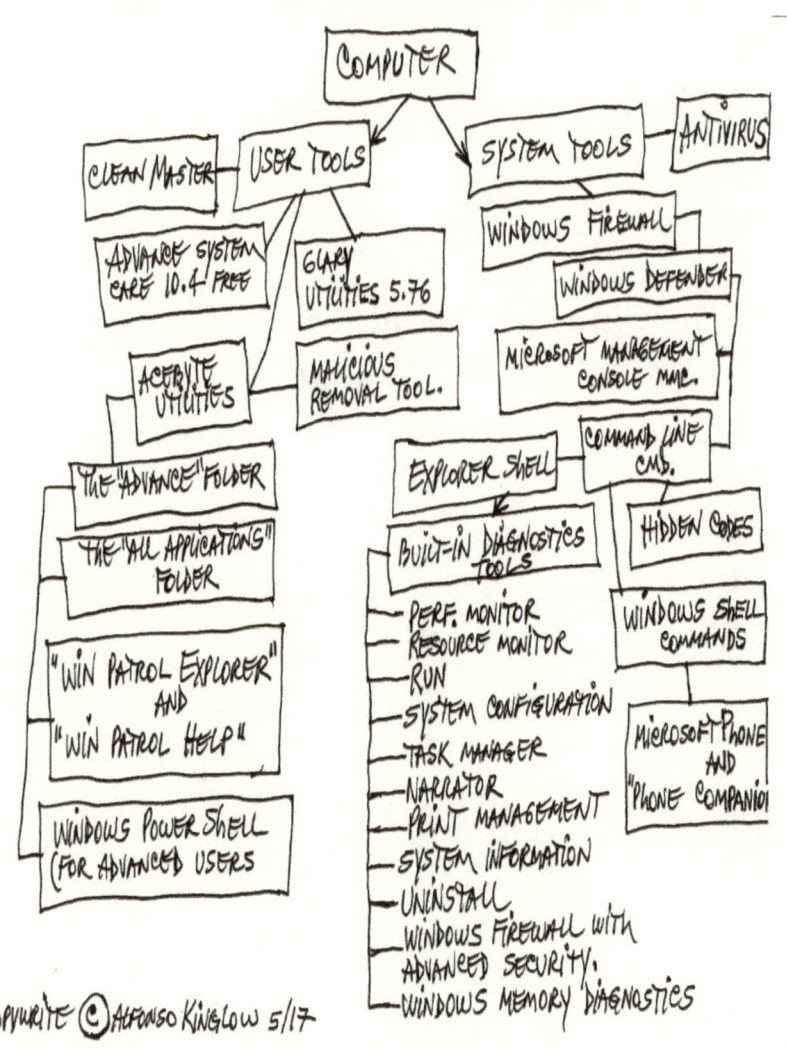

COMPUTER

CLEAN MASTER

USER TOOLS

SYSTEM TOOLS

ANTIVIRUS

ADVANCE SYSTEM CARE 10.4 FREE

GLARY UTILITIES 5.76

ACEBYTE UTILITIES

MALICIOUS REMOVAL TOOL.

WINDOWS FIREWALL

WINDOWS DEFENDER

MICROSOFT MANAGEMENT CONSOLE MMC.

THE "ADVANCE" FOLDER

THE "ALL APPLICATIONS" FOLDER

"WIN PATROL EXPLORER" AND "WIN PATROL HELP"

WINDOWS POWER SHELL (FOR ADVANCED USERS

EXPLORER SHELL

COMMAND LINE CMD.

BUILT-IN DIAGNOSTICS TOOLS

HIDDEN CODES

- PERF. MONITOR
- RESOURCE MONITOR
- RUN
- SYSTEM CONFIGURATION
- TASK MANAGER
- NARRATOR
- PRINT MANAGEMENT
- SYSTEM INFORMATION
- UNINSTALL
- WINDOWS FIREWALL WITH ADVANCED SECURITY.
- WINDOWS MEMORY DIAGNOSTICS

WINDOWS SHELL COMMANDS

MICROSOFT PHONE AND "PHONE COMPANION

COPYWRITE © ALFONSO KINGLOW 5/17

COMPUTER VIRUSSES.—

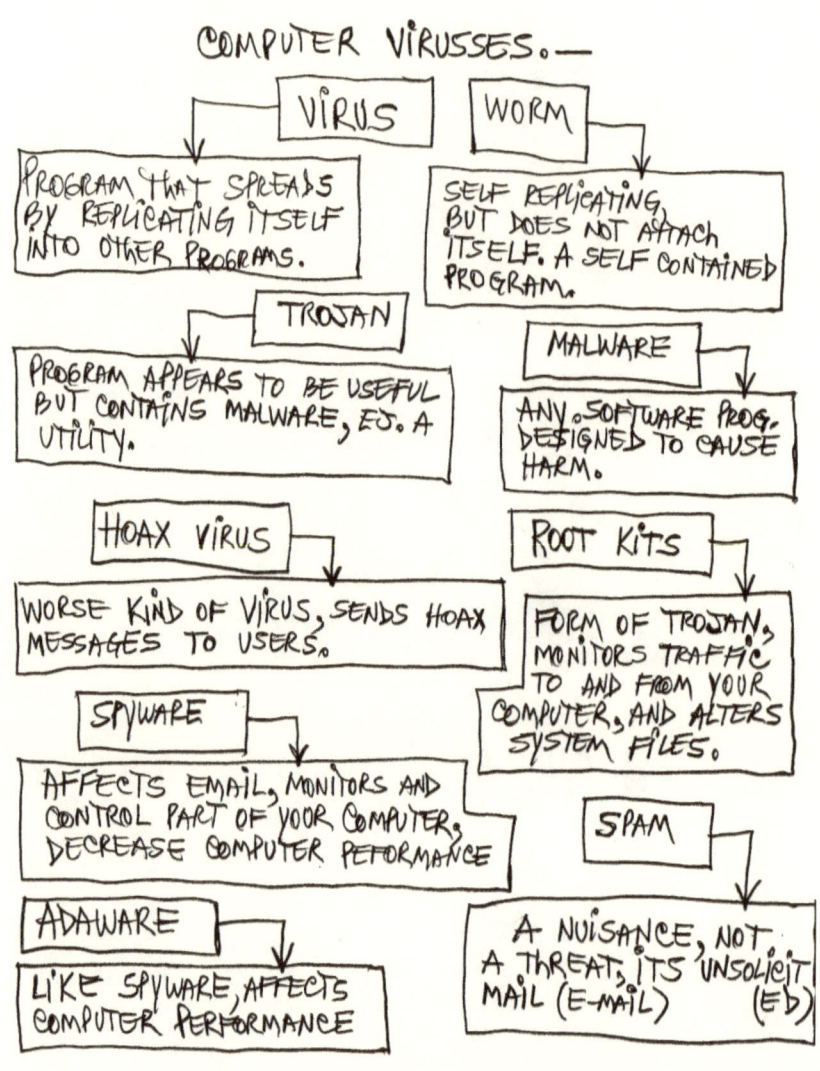

VIRUS — PROGRAM THAT SPREADS BY REPLICATING ITSELF INTO OTHER PROGRAMS.

WORM — SELF REPLICATING, BUT DOES NOT ATTACH ITSELF. A SELF CONTAINED PROGRAM.

TROJAN — PROGRAM APPEARS TO BE USEFUL BUT CONTAINS MALWARE, EJ. A UTILITY.

MALWARE — ANY SOFTWARE PROG. DESIGNED TO CAUSE HARM.

HOAX VIRUS — WORSE KIND OF VIRUS, SENDS HOAX MESSAGES TO USERS.

ROOT KITS — FORM OF TROJAN, MONITORS TRAFFIC TO AND FROM YOUR COMPUTER, AND ALTERS SYSTEM FILES.

SPYWARE — AFFECTS EMAIL, MONITORS AND CONTROL PART OF YOUR COMPUTER, DECREASE COMPUTER PEFORMANCE

SPAM — A NUISANCE, NOT A THREAT, ITS UNSOLICIT MAIL (E-MAIL) (ED)

ADAWARE — LIKE SPYWARE, AFFECTS COMPUTER PERFORMANCE

2016 COPYWRITE © ALFONSO J. KING/DIN

NEW WI-FI STANDARD. _____

From Huawei. Internet Source.

The New Wi-Fi Standard That Will Make the
802.11AC Obsolete.__

The first wave of 802.11ac routers currently available on the market are based on earlier drafts of the 802.11ac standard and will no longer be the fastest standard on the market. The second wave of 802.11ac devices are based on the final ratified standard and are set to include new features that better optimize wireless networks.

802.11AC Standard: Wave 1 vs. Wave 2

802.11ac Wave 2 is set to include MU-MIMO capabilities among other advances that will give routers a speed boost from the original 3.47 Gbps in first generation to 6.93 Gbps in the final iteration of the standard.

MU-MIMO or Multiple-user multiple input/multiple output "enables [routers] to send multiple spatial streams to multiple clients

simultaneously". With 160 MHz channel bonding (as opposed to 80 Mhz bonding over wave 1) and

backwards compatibility with previous standards, the new standard boasts a performance boost over the first generation of 802.11ac routers. With a physical link rate of nearly 7 Gbps, users hoping to upgrade to 802.11ac should consider waiting to catch the second wave.

Market Trends

Dell'Oro Group has published a report that notes that the "Wireless LAN (WLAN) market grew eight percent in the third quarter 2014 versus the year-ago period" and that "Enterprise-class 802.11ac-based radio access points grew a robust 40 percent versus the second quarter 2014."

The report forecasts that the WLAN market will be stimulated with the release of 802.11ac Wave 2 equipment along with government funding in the US meant to support wireless connectivity in schools and libraries.

The New Standard 802.11ax

But even the second generation of the 802.11ac standard cannot compare with the wireless speeds of a still newer specification. The 802.11ax standard is set to "not just increase the overall speed of a network"but to "quadruple wireless speeds of individual clients." Huawei's research and development labs , have reported to successfully reach wireless connections speeds of 10 Gbps utilizing the 5GHz frequency band.

The standard is set to be finalized in 2019, but manufacturers can be expected to release products based on the pre-standard as early as 2018.

While wireless connections keep getting faster, the options for internet users to connect to the internet keep expanding. In the near future, users can be expected to connect to the internet using LED lights, or gain wireless access to the internet by connecting to a micro-satellite orbiting the Earth.

USB 3.0 and 3.1 New Standard. __

Source: Public Domain/Open Source

Networx™ USB 3.0 SuperSpeed Cables combine style, quality, performance and value to give a great deal on a great USB cable. The molded connectors are designed to make them easy to grip. Networx™ USB 3.0 cables are double-shielded with a dual foil and braid. The connector is surrounded by a metal shield and the cable braid is also soldered to the connector to create an end-to-end full shielding solution guaranteeing a noise-free connection. SuperSpeed USB 3.0 is 2nd revision of the ubiquitous USB (Universal Serial Bus) Standard. Clocking in at speeds up to 5 Gbit/s, USB 3.0 is a vast improvement over the USB 2.0 speed of 400 Mbit/s while being completely backwards compatible with USB 2.0.

32.   USB 3.0 A Male to A Female

33.   Up to 5Gbit/sec

34.   PC and Mac Compatible

35.   Ultra-flexible jacket; Molded strain relief

36.   Foil and braid shield to guarantee an interference free connection

37.   Proper current to your USB device via Heavy-duty 24AWG power wire

38.   EMI/RFI int: Metal connector shield to meet FCC requirements

USB 3.0

USB 3.0 is the third major version of the Universal Serial Bus standard for interfacing computers and electronic devices. Among other improvements, USB 3.0 adds the new transfer rate referred to as SuperSpeed USB that can transfer data at up to 5 Gbit/s, which is about 10 times as fast as the USB 2.0 standard.

Manufacturers are recommended to distinguish USB 3.0 connectors from their USB 2.0 counterparts by blue color-coding of the Standard-A receptacles and plugs, and by the initials SS.

USB 3.0 SuperSpeed Cables combine
style, quality, performance and value to
give a great deal on a great USB cable. The
molded connectors are designed to make
them easy to grip. Networx™ USB 3.0
cables are double-shielded with a dual foil
and braid. The connector is surrounded by
a metal shield and the cable braid is also
soldered to the connector to create an end-
to-end full shielding solution guaranteeing
a noise-free connection.

SuperSpeed USB 3.0 is 2nd revision of the ubiquitous USB (Universal Serial Bus) Standard. Clocking in at speeds up to 5 Gbit/s, USB 3.0 is a vast improvement over the USB 2.0 speed of 400 Mbit/s while being completely backwards compatible with USB 2.0.

18.   USB 3.0 A Male to B Male
19.   Up to 5Gbit/sec
20.   PC and Mac Compatible
21.   Ultra-flexible jacket; Molded strain relief
22.   Foil and braid shield to guarantee an interference free connection
23.   Proper current to your USB device via Heavy-duty 24AWG power wire

24.   EMI/RFI interference: Metal connector shield to meet FCC requirements

BEST SEARCH ENGINES ON THE INTERNET USING BRIDGE, PORTALS AND GATEWAYS.

Google

Yahoo

Bing

Baidu (China)

Ask.com

Dogpile- Semantic

DuckDuckgo- Semantic

Yippy

Google Scholar

Webopedia

Torch

TouchGraph

Ecosia

Blekko

Gigablast- Open Source

Topsy

SocialMention

Whos Talkin

Scribd- Books

Pronto

Wolframalpha

Internet Archive.org

Yandex.ru (Russia)

USED BY THE WEB (WWW.)

Protocols: Set of Rules that are used when two connections communicate. Can not be changed or modified.

Gateways: A network node or connection that connects two Networks using Different Protocols. (Appletalk -TCP/IP – FTP – ARP – PPP).

Bridge: Connects a LAN (Local Area Network) to another LAN, using the same Protocol.

Portal: Website serving as an entry point to the Internet with many links, data resources, emails, news, weather , etc..

CHAPTER THREE

Protecting your Computer from Viruses.__

You can protect your computer by installing a free or paid version of an Antivirus program. Many Antivirus programs are available from different manufacturers, they all protect your computer when properly installed, and with the Virus Definition file updated. A first time Scan is required before the program can begin to protect your computer. Before you start the next Scan, after you have done your first Scan, make sure that you are disconnected from the Internet, and or turn off momentarily your router. Then you may Scan your computer again.

The first time you Scan your computer you need to be connected to the Internet so that your Virus Definition file can get updated.

It is advisable to Scan your computer at least once a week.

A Security software program is not an Antivirus program and does not offer any protection against the many viruses that are a threat. Some Security software programs claim to protect your computer from viruses, only an Antivirus software program will protect your computer from viruses.

Your Computer Security. ___

Windows 7 and 8 comes with some security protection. The new Windows 10 operating system have a new complete security configuration that is presented here as part of the Revision.

They are two main Security modules in the Control Panel, one of them is called; Windows Defender and the other is Windows Firewall. Make sure that they are both turned on and are working. Your Firewall must be always on to protect your computer from threats.

Firewalls can be internal or external, and can be software and or hardware. Having an external Firewall box will greatly enhance the security protection to your computer.

The Control Panel in Windows 7 - 8 and 10.

The Control Panel is the heart of your computer. All the modules running in the Control Panel are performing a function so that your computer may run smoothly.

To access the Control Panel, go to the Start or Run button in the lower left side of your Desktop, and select Settings, if the Control Panel is not visible in the menu, to bring up the Control Panel or if you are running Windows 8 you may also go to the Folder on the lower left side of your Desktop, and click on Computer, and the Control Panel will be displayed in the center Tabs that are visible. The Control Panel Icon Folder is unique and very different from any other folders.

Administrative Users vs. Standard Users

In the Control Panel one of the most important controls is the User's Control Panel, where you can Create new Users for your computer and edit existing users. It is recommended that you

first create a New User, when you get your computer for the first time. This New User would most likely be you. Once the user is created, you need to give the New User Administrative Rights, so that the user may have full control of the Computer. This user will then become the User Administrator. A Standard User will not have rights and privileges on the computer to do anything. As the Owner of your computer, you need to have full rights on your machine. Otherwise you will not be able to install or remove any software or do basic maintenance on your own machine, so this is a very first most important step, after getting your computer.

System Administrator vs. User

Administrator

It is very important to know what is the System Administrator Password. If the Windows System Software gets corrupted, and needs to be re-installed; you will need to know the Administrator Password in order to get into the System to perform general maintenance and re

installation of the system software. When Windows is installed for the first time on any machine, in the installation process, a password is requested for the *Administrator*, this password is important to know and remember, if you did not install your system and some one else did it; then you might be out of luck if you do not know the Administrator Password or Admin password. Most computers come with the Windows OS already installed, so the Admin password is not known. It is therefore important to get the original Windows Re-installation DVD, so that you may reinstall Windows if it gets corrupted or crashes.

Every new Computer should be provided with the Installation DVD included in the "sealed" Box and not in a Box with a Tape over it, which indicates that the Box was opened, and that the original DVD, Manuals and other User Documentation was taken out. Please note this as it is obvious that the Computer was not shipped to the store in a box with a Tape around it. All Computers are shipped in
"sealed" boxes, there is no Tape involved.

The User Administrator only has rights and privileges over the user's machine and does not have any System administrator rights over any of the System software.

If the user tries to change, alter, modify etc..
Any system applications; a message will be

displayed alerting the "User" that he or she does not have any rights or privilege to make or do the changes they want.

Please note that the User with Administrative privileges is not the same as the User Administrator.

DR ALFONSO J. KINGLOW

CHAPTER FOUR

COMPUTER NETWORKS, NETWORKING AND THE COMPUTER NETWORK CARDS OR ADAPTERS.

Let us define what Computer Networks are first, any computer that is connected to any other computer to share files and other applications is said to be connected to a Network. When computers need to share files and other software they are connected together in a LAN. A LAN is a Local Area Network. To facilitate this configuration, all computers have built in Network Cards.

They are two kinds of Network Cards also called NIC's, The first card or NIC is the " Ethernet Card" This is a special card that meets the International Standard for Networking called Ethernet (IEE 802.3) or Project 802, which is an IEEE Standard, accepted worldwide. The speed of this network card is 100 Mbps or 1 Gbps.,(Gigabit Ethernet) or higher.

The Gigabit Ethernet card is much faster than the 100 Mbps card and is desirable.

WIRELESS CARD OR ADAPTER. __

The second Network card is the Wireless card or WiFi card (802.11b/g/n) and the new standard ac/ and /ad.

So the built in Wireless card should be (802.11 b/g/n or 802.11 b/g/n/AC or AD. This is the new Wireless Standard for the Network Card that is preferred, a new Standard is been developed and will be available in 2019; if you want to have a fast Network connection. If your Wireless card does not meet this standard, then it will be very slow and you will not be able to connect to the Internet. Your Wireless built in card must be at least (802.11 b/g/n) or higher.

Computers connect to the Internet through these cards. The connection to and from these cards is called Networking.

The settings for your Wireless and Ethernet cards are in the Control Panel, and it's called: "Networking and Sharing Center".

Networking is divided into LAN (Local Area Networks) and WAN (Wide

Area Networks The largest WAN in the world is the Internet.

Wireless adapters or cards are also installed into Printers which makes them " Wireless Printers" Most printers are now Wireless and require no cables, most printers are supplied with a USB (Universal Serial Bus) Cable, which is another Standard used in computers and networking.

WAN Networking requires special equipment and meets different standards with different kinds of cables and interfaces.

THE NETWORKING MODEL

Networking is based on a Model accepted worldwide; it's called the OSI Networking Model or Open Systems Interconnect. Computer Network cards and Networking in general must follow this Model. All network cards are assigned a network protocol number or network ID that identifies the card on the Network. It is a special hexadecimal number (numbers and letters combined), this is also called in networking an IP

(Internet Protocol) Address. This IP identifies the computer on a Network and is part of the Internet Protocol (TCP/IP) a Networking Standard. Without a TCP/IP address number the computer can not connect to the Internet or Network.

The speed of the computer Internet connection will depend on the built in Network cards. To find out what kind of Network cards is installed in your computer; go to the Control Panel to Network and Sharing Center and select "change adapter settings" to display the type and kind of network cards installed in the computer.

Networks and the Internet. ____

Networks are used to join computers and devices together and to share resources.

The type of resources that are shared are: Information, Hardware, Software, and Data.

A Hardware resource that is shared could be a

single connected Printer, that is shared via the Network to multiple Computers. These are shared through a LAN (Local Area Network) or a WAN (Wide Area Network.)

To access the Internet services the user can connect via an ISP (Internet Service Provider) or via an OSP (Online Service Provider).

The main Internet Service is the World Wide Web (WWW.) and the Internet is the largest Network in the World.

The Internet is a worldwide collection of Networks that links individuals with resources and Data. The Internet have Millions of users and is growing more and more every day. The Web contains Billions of Documents called Web Pages.

The Internet Web Page Link. ___

A Web Page on the Internet may link to other Web Documents, and to Text, Graphics, Sound and Video.

A Web site (Google) may contain a collection of related Web Pages. Computers store Web Pages and the user, can use a Web Browser such as IE (Internet Explorer) or Firefox to view them.

The content of those Web Pages can be: Financial Data, News, Guides, Weather, Legal Information, other..

A very important Web document or link is: " The
Future of Internet 2) a New Technology and
Standard for the Internet under Development by
the World Wide Web Consortium (WWWC.)
and/or W3C.

STOP WINDOWS 10 UPDATES FROM FORCING UPDATES ON YOUR COMPUTER. ____

Option 1: Stop The Windows Update Service

As central as it is to the core of Windows 10, Windows Update is actually just another Windows process so it can be stopped with these simple steps:

- Open the Run command (Win + R), in it type: services.msc and press enter
- From the Services list which appears find the Windows Update service and open it
- In 'Startup Type' (under the 'General' tab) change it to 'Disabled'

- Restart

To re-enable Windows Update simply repeat these four steps, but change the Startup Type to 'Automatic'

OPTION 2:

Press the Windows logo key + R then type gpedit.msc and click OK. Go to Computer Configuration > Administrative Templates > Windows Components > Windows Update. Select Disabled in Configured Automatic Updates on the left, and click Apply and OK to disable the Windows automatic update feature.

CHAPTER FIVE

A List of Common Computer Acronyms

Source: 22 Bevis Marks, London EC3A 7JB | 020 8501 7676 | www.ouritdept.co.uk | info@ouritdept.co.uk Facebook /LondonITSupport | Twitter @ouritdepartment

Learning about computers requires you to become familiar with a series of acronyms that refer to various aspects of computer technology.

The list of computer acronyms used to describe various components can be overwhelming if you are just beginning to understand the world of computer science. To help you focus on the most significant terms, we have organized a list of computer acronyms to help you get started.

AD – Active Directory: AD is a Microsoft directory service with a domain controller. The controller authenticates and authorizes a set of processes and services accessed by users and computers running on a Windows Server operating system and domain network.

AI – Artificial Intelligence: AI refers to the intelligence displayed by any computing devices or software that is capable of exhibiting intelligent behavior.

AIFF - Audio Interchange File Format: AIFF is a common audio format developed by Apple Corporation and is used as a standard format for storing and transmitting audio samples.

AMOLED - Active-Matrix Organic Light-Emitting Diode: AMOLED is a type of power saving display technology commonly used in mobile devices. The technology is comprised of an active matrix of organic light-emitting diode (OLED) pixels integrated with a TFT (Thin-Film Transistor) array which controls electrical currents being transmitted to each individual pixel within the device display.

API - Application Program Interface: API is a technology used to create software applications using a group of set protocols and routines that define the functionality of the software.

ASCII - American Standard Code for Information Interchange: ASCII is a format used for text files in both UNIX and DOS operating systems. The files consist of 7-bit binary numbers that represent a numeric, alphabetic, or special character within the code. The purpose of the files are to support specific functions within an operating system.

AVI - Audio Visual Interleave: AVI is a Microsoft container format which stores both audio and video files to allow the playback of audio with video.

B

BIOS - Basic Input/Output System: BIOS refers to the firmware installed in all personal computers and is an important part of the boot up process. The BIOS is the first component that runs when you start up a computer and also allows the user to control the manner in which the computer boots up.

BMP – Bitmap: BMP is a simple graphics file format used on computers running the Windows operating system. The BMP file format is not compressed and typically large in size. This means the format cannot be used for transmitting images over the Internet.

BPS – Bits per Second: BPS is a computing bit rate which defines the number of bits that are transmitted over a specified unit of time. Bits per second determines the connection speed of computers and communications technology.

BYOD – Bring Your Own Device: BYOD is a policy used in business environments that permits employees to use their own computers and mobile devices in the workplace. BYOD policies are put in place to keep sensitive information safe while improving employee productivity.

C

CD-R - Compact Disc Recordable: A CD-R is a compact disc that can be written to in a single instance and then read at random multiple times.

CD-ROM - Compact Disc Read-Only Memory: A CD-ROM is a compact disc that digitally stores data that can be accessed using your computer. CDROMS are not writable and you cannot erase the data, hence the Read-Only Memory described in the term CD-ROM.

CD-RW - Compact Disc Re-Writable: CD-RW is a compact disc that can be written to, erased, and then written to again multiple times. It is commonly used as a means for backing up and storing files and data.

CPU - Central Processing Unit: A CPU is the electronic circuit board inside a computer and is responsible for carrying out instructions delivered by a computer application. The instructions involve performing the logic, arithmetic equations and I/O (input/output) as specified by the program.

D

DDR - Double Data Rate: DDR refers to a category of memory integrated circuits built into a computer system. The DDR technology facilitates higher data transfer rates when compared to SDR (Single Data Rate) and by using stringent control of electrical data and clock signal timing. The different classes of DDR include DDR1, DDR2, DDR3, and most recently, DDR4. DDR is commonly referred to as synchronous dynamic random-access memory or DDR SDRAM.

DLL - Dynamic Link Library: DLL is a shared library system of files used with the Windows operating system. The code contained in a DLL file is shared among all processes which rely on a specific DLL file to operate. This means they inhabit a single location in the physical memory which in turn, saves on space while improving functionality and efficiency.

DMA - Direct Memory Access: DMA is a program included in computer operating systems which assists the Central Processing Unit (CPU) when the CPU is unable to keep up with data transfer rates or is challenged with slow data transfer for Input/Output (I/O). Direct Memory Access sanctions a specific hardware subsystem to independently access the primary Random Access Memory (RAM) separately from the CPU. This allows the CPU to perform other tasks while the data transfer is taking place.

DNS - Domain Name System: A DNS is used to identify devices connected to the Internet by using a unique IP (Internet Protocol) address. The IP address for each device or website location is translated into a domain such as anyname.com which is easier for users to remember instead of entering the numeric IP address version to access a website. The DNS also acts as a directory service or type of phone book for all devices connected to the Internet to facilitate ease of communications.

DOS - Disk Operating System: The term DOS refers an early IBM operating system prior to the inception of Windows. The DOS operating system utilises a command line to perform tasks and access applications and was partially present in the early Windows operating systems (95 and 98). Currently, PC technicians use DOS commands to perform computer repairs and to work with settings within the operating system.

DRAM - Dynamic Random Access Memory: DRAM

is the main memory in laptops, tablets, desktops, and workstation devices. It is responsible for storing frequently accessed data and applications to provide the user with faster access while performing computing tasks. DRAM offers a simple design with only one capacitor and transistor used for each bit of data. It also provides enhanced performance by using separate capacitors to store one bit of data in an integrated circuit.

DVD-R Digital Versatile Disc Recordable: DVD-R is a storage format for digital optical discs. The letter "R" means that the DVD disc can be recorded to in one instance and then read at random multiple times.

DVD-RW - Digital Versatile Disk Rewritable: DVDRW is an optical disc storage format which allows you to record information to a disc and rewrite it multiple times. The advantage over the DVD-R format is you can erase the data as many times as you want and then rewrite, as opposed to only being able to record once as in a DVD-R format.

DVI - Digital Visual Interface: DVI is a technology which offers a digital interface used to connect a computer monitor or other display device. The technology facilitates the transfer of digital video to the display device and is connected to and operates on a unified video standard to ensure device compatibility.

E

EDI - Electronic Data Interchange: EDI is a standard used for electronic communications to transfer structured data between two devices, companies, or users in different areas of the world. The standard ensures documents can be opened and read when exchanged with devices of different operating systems and applications.

EGA – Enhanced Graphics Adapter: EGA is a standard established by IBM (International Business Machines) which specifies the type of computer display. EGA defines the display colour and the type of resolution and supports an array of bit colour specifications and pixel aspect ratios.

EULA – End User License Agreement: A EULA is a contract used by software licensors that defines to the end user how the software can be used. It is used to protect the copyrights of the software vendor and to establish parameters for the licensed copy of the software.

F

FAT – File Allocation Table: FAT refers to a specific architecture for a computer file system. The files are commonly found on external storage devices and provide enhanced performance for all types of operating systems. FAT files were originally found on hard disks when DOS was an operating system but, is no longer used as a main file system in

Windows operating systems. Instead, FAT files act as the default file system for external storage devices.

FTP - File Transfer Protocol: FTP is a protocol which is used to transfer files over the Internet. The files are transferred from one host to another using a network or Internet connection. Website managers frequently use FTP to upload files from a computer to a server where the website is stored.

FXP - File Exchange Protocol: FXP is the process of transferring data from one server to the other while bypassing a device connection. The method is used by network administrators to provide access to data and resources stored on each server when working in different locations.

G

GIF - Graphics Interchange Format: GIF is a graphics image format widely used on the Internet. It is a convenient format due to its versatility and support for different browsers and operating systems. The images are in bitmap image format and are compressed for easy downloading when accessing web pages.

GPS - Global Positioning System: GPS is a navigation system used to determine a current location. A GPS system is satellite-based and comprised of a satellite network located in orbit powered by a radio signals. GPS systems can be used as a standalone device for guidance when travelling or they can be located in mobile phones and other portable devices.

GPU - Graphics Processing Unit: A GPU is an electronic circuit located inside your computer that helps to speed up the production of images to enable them to be viewed on a display screen. GPUs are built into a large variety of devices including laptops, mobile devices, gaming consoles, and more, to facilitate the processing or graphics and images.

GUI - Graphical User Interface: A GUI is a technology that facilitates interaction between electronic devices using image icons as opposed to text commands. A GUI is typically present in portable devices, gaming devices, and media players and works through the modification of visual indicators.

H

HTML - Hypertext Markup Language: HTML is a markup language which is designed to be read by web browsers such as Internet Explorer, Mozilla, Google Chrome, and others. The language is used to design web pages and describes how objects and text should appear when the page is viewed in a web browser.

HTTP - Hypertext Transfer Protocol: HTTP is a standard protocol used for data communications on the Internet. The standard is used for request and response such as when you type in a website domain address to access a specific website. Your browser is requesting access to the website and the server responds by displaying the web page.

HTTPS - Hypertext Transport Protocol Secure: Similar to HTTP, HTTPS is a standard protocol used for data communication in the form of request and response. The difference is HTTPS provides a secure connection, often symbolised by a padlock, from your browser to a server to protect sensitive information such as the transfer of credit card data when you make an online purchase.

I

IEEE Institute Of Electrical And Electronics Engineers: The IEEE is an organisation that consists of members of the Institute of Radio Engineers and the American Institute of Electrical Engineers. The primary purpose of IEEE is to define standards for electronic and wireless communications to create a global uniform standard that allows devices of all types to connect to electronics and wireless technologies.

IGP – Interior Gateway Protocol: IGP is a standard protocol which is used for routing data between multiple Local Area Networks (LAN). The data is then used by an IP network protocol to determine how data transmissions should be routed within the network.

IM - Instant Message: IM is the process of sending text messages in real-time using an Internet connection. The messages can also be transmitted within an organisation over a Local Area Network

-

(LAN). IM is also known as online chat and involves sending short messages over a network connection.

ISP - Internet Service Provider: An ISP is a provider of Internet connection services to provide businesses and individual households with access to the Internet. ISPs typically use an array of technologies such as satellite or cable to offer Internet access to their customers.

J

JPEG Joint Photographic Experts Group: JPEG is a digital image format commonly used in digital photography. The JPEG format is a lossy compression format and is the most commonly used format for transmitting images over the Internet.

JRE - Java Runtime Environment: A JRE works with the Java Virtual Machine which hosts valid class files created in the Java Virtual Machine language. Java is a programming language that supports many objects embedded in websites. Without JRE, some of the website components may not work unless Java is installed on your computer from the Sun Microsystems Java website.

K

KB – Kilobyte: KB refers to a unit of digital information. One KB is the equivalent of 1000 bytes and refers to a specific file size of information.

KBPS - Kilobits Per Second: KBPS refers to a specific rate of data transfer over a network connection. One kilobit is the equivalent to 1000 bits per second

-

which is a slower connection than Mbps (megabits per second) and GBps (gigabytes per second).

L

LAN - Local Area Network: A LAN is a network that connects a series of computers together to enable the devices to communicate with one another. Local Area Networks are limited to a specific area such as a business, corporation, school, or other. Devices outside of the LAN are unable to use the LAN to connect with devices on the LAN.

LCD - Liquid Crystal Display: LCD refers to a display that contains liquid crystal properties. LCD displays can include televisions, digital signage, computer monitors, and more. The liquid crystals do not directly give off light and instead, use light modulation properties for energy efficiency.

M

MAC Media Access Control Address: MAC is a type of communication protocol which provides channel access and addressing to control devices. The technology enables multiple terminals to communicate with a shared medium network that provides multiple access. The hardware which is used for MAC is known as a Media Access Controller.

MBPS - Megabits per Second: MBPS refers to the speed of data being transferred over a network and is measured in megabits. One megabit represents over one million bits which means the data transfer rate is one million bits per second. This is right in between Kbps (kilobits per second) and GBps (gigabits per second).

MIDI - Musical Instrument Digital Interface: MIDI is a standard protocol used to connect computers with musical instruments. The protocol allows you to connect a music instrument to a computer to work with pitch, sequence recording, volume, tempos, musical notation, and other musical techniques.

N

NFS – Network File System: NFS is a file system protocol that allows an end user to access network files from a client computer. When the protocol is

-

implemented on a network, any device connected to the network can access and share files.

NIC - Network Interface Card: A NIC is a hardware component which is embedded into a computer to provide the device with access to a network. NICs operate on multiple queues for transmission and reception. When data packets are received by the NIC, each packet is assigned to a specific queue to improve performance during data transmission.

O

OEM Original Equipment Manufacturer: AN OEM is a company that manufactures a specific part for computers. For example, if your computer is equipped with an Intel processor but the computer make is Acer, Intel is the OEM for the Central Processing Unit (CPU).

OLE - Object Linking and Embedding: OLE is a technology that allows the user to embed documents within an application for the purpose of editing. OLE was created by Microsoft and is used to import different types of data and information from different applications.

OLED – Organic Light-Emitting Diode: OLED is a technology that contains light emitting diodes that give off light via a current of electricity. OLED technology is used in a variety of displays and does not require any backlighting. The technology increases black levels and provides for a display construction that is much thinner than an LCD display.

P

P2P – Peer-To-Peer: P2P is a specific type of architecture which consists of applications designed to distribute workloads among peers. Each peer is considered an equal contributor to the application on a peer-to-peer network. An example of a P2P architecture was the file sharing system known as Napster, which allows members of the P2P to freely share files without the need for server coordination.

PC - Personal Computer: PC is a term used to describe a computer designed to accommodate individual users. A PC is operated directly and personally owned by the end user without any third party intervention.

PDF - Portable Document Format: PDF is a universal document format used to transmit documents to any device with any type of operating system. The primary purpose of PDF is to ensure documents can be read by the recipient in a fixed layout that ensures the document displays properly.

PNG - Portable Network Graphic: PNG is a graphic format which serves as an alternative to the GIF image format. The file contains raster graphics, is compatible with lossless data compression, and utilises 24-bit RGB colours and 32-bit RGBA colours in addition to grayscale images.

PPI - Pixels per Inch: PPI is a method used to measure the resolution or pixel density of a digital image component such as a television screen or computer monitor. PPI can also be used to measure the pixel density of a specific image file and uses vertical and horizontal density as part of the measurement.

R

RAID - Redundant Array of Independent Disks: RAID is method of backup storage that is comprised of multiple hard drive devices combined into a single unit for the purpose of data protection. When data is backed up, it is distributed across multiple drives (also known as redundancy) so if one drive fails, the data can be accessed on an alternative disk drive.

RAM - Random Access Memory: RAM is a computer component that stores data and applications that are frequently accessed by the user. This allows data and applications to be accessed quickly and prevents the computer from having to go back to the hard drive to retrieve the requested information.

ROM - Read-Only Memory: ROM refers to a type of data storage which is used by a computer or other device. The term is commonly used as CD-ROM in which the data can be read on the disc but cannot be modified.

RTF - Rich Text Format: RTF is a Microsoft document file format that can be opened using a variety of different word processing applications. The format supports images and text style formatting which remains unchanged when viewed in an application other than Microsoft Word.

S

SAN - Storage Area Network: A SAN is used to access files and data via a dedicated network of multiple storage devices. The technology is used to manage optical storage, disk arrays and other storage resources connected to a server. When the SAN network becomes accessible on the server, the storage devices appear as though they are an included component in each individual computer connected to the network.

SATA - Serial Advanced Technology Attachment: SATA is a technology that establishes a connection to optical and hard drives using a computer bus interface. The interface is responsible for connecting host bus adapter to the optical or hard drive or other type of mass storage device. The advantage of this technology is to provide faster data transfer and smaller cable sizes at a reduced cost.

SDRAM - Synchronous Dynamic Random Access Memory: SDRAM is a widely used technology in computers and is considered to be DRAM. The only difference is the DRAM synchronises with the system bus which is responsible for connecting major computer system components. The end result is improved data access that is faster and more efficient than conventional Random Access Memory (RAM).

SMS - Short Message Service: SMS is a method used to transmit short messages over the Internet or via a mobile communication system. The technology is used on modern day smartphones, in addition to personal computers and tablets.

SQL - Structured Query Language: SQL is a programming language used by database developers to enable the management of data in a relational database management system. SQL is a standard programming language designed to be transferrable to different database configurations without requiring code modification.

SRAM - Static Random Access Memory: In contrast with DRAM which requires refreshment on a periodic basis, Static Random Access memory does not require this process. This is what makes the technology and data access much faster via a connection to the CPU (Central Processing Unit) cache as opposed to the main memory of the computer.

SSID - Service Set Identifier: An SSID is a service set that assists with the identification of a specific wireless network. The identifier locates the origin of a device connected to a wireless network, in addition to the wireless access point.

SSL - Secure Sockets Layer: SSL is used to ensure secure communications over a network such as the Internet. The protocol uses cryptography to encrypt data being transmitted between two parties. This includes personal information, credit card numbers, banking transactions, and other sensitive data. The technology is frequently used in conjunction with HTTPS.

T

TCP/IP - Transmission Control Protocol/Internet Protocol: TCP/IP is a protocol used to determine how data transmission should be addressed, packetized and routed to a specific point of destination. It is an important standard protocol used for successful communications over the Internet.

TIFF - Tagged Image File Format: TIFF is a common image file format designed for the exchange of raster graphics between different applications. The file format is frequently used in medical imaging, desktop publishing, and 3-D applications.

U

UPNP - Universal Plug And Play: UPNP is a technology that allows the devices connected to your home network to discover one another and access specific services. Typically, UPNP is used to stream media between two different devices and allows you to discontinue a program on one device and then pick it up on a second device in another room.

URL - Uniform Resource Locator: A URL is also known as a website address and is the domain address you type into your browser to access a specific website. URLs are also present on the Search Engine Results Page (SERP) and contain a link that leads you to the website.

USB - Universal Serial Bus: USB is a technology that defines various protocols included in a serial bus component. The protocols, in addition to the connectors and cables, are used to facilitate communications between computers and peripheral devices such as USB flash drives, headphones, external hard drives, portable media players, and more.

V

VGA - Video Graphics Array: VGA is an IBM graphics standard used to deliver high definition video. The technology exists within a television screen or computer monitor and is designed to handle 1080p resolutions or higher.

VoIP - Voice over Internet Protocol: VoIP refers to a method of communication using an IP (Internet Protocol) network. VoIP is commonly associated with IP telephony which offers telephone communication using an Internet connection. VoIP is available on many different types of devices and typically uses the Skype VoIP application to establish a telephone or video communication over the Internet.

VPN - Virtual Private Network: A VPN is a private network which is accessed using traffic encryption or virtual tunneling protocols. Although the network uses an Internet connection for remote access, the encryption technologies and security policies provide secure access. VPNs are frequently used by remote workers and other professionals that require a secure connection when performing computing tasks.

W

WAN - Wide Area Network: A WAN is a network that is spread over a large geographical area and is connected via telecommunications lines that are leased. A WAN commonly refers to the Internet but also can consist of a series of networks from different geographical locations, such as those for government entities, corporations, and others.

WEP - Wired Equivalent Privacy: WEP is a wireless protocol that is used to secure the transmission of data over a network. The technology uses encryption under the 802.11 wireless standard developed by the IEEE to establish a secure network connection from any device connected to a specific network.

WPA - Wi-Fi Protected Access: WPA is often identified as WPA and WPA2 which are security certifications developed to provide enhanced security to wireless networks. WPA was developed as an alternative to WEP which was found to have vulnerabilities in the technology, and uses an encryption mode certified by the Wi-Fi Alliance.

WWW - World Wide Web: The World Wide Web is commonly referred to as the Internet and is a large network where users access a wealth of documents and other information available via websites, hypertext links, videos, and more. It is also a place where users with an Internet connection can download software applications, make purchases, take online classes, and access a wealth of other helpful resources.

X

XHTML - Extensible Hypertext Markup Language: Similar to HTML, XHTML is a markup language used to create websites that can be viewed by a web browser. The difference is XHTML provides extended versions of HTML which increases the ability of HTML to integrate with other data formats. This allows for easier access to more advanced applications and website components.

XML - Extensible Markup Language: XML is a format which defines parameters for encoding documents. It is a type of markup language used to read documents on the Internet and makes the documents readable by a machine or human. 22

Z

ZIP: ZIP stands for speed and is a compressed archive file format used to transmit large files over a network connection. ZIP files use lossless data compression to save disk space using compression algorithms. The format is convenient when transmitting large files. When the compressed format is used, it is possible to transmit multiple large files within one ZIP file without experiencing lag time during transmission. When the recipient receives the file, the file in unzipped for viewing using a program such as WinZip or other.

CHAPTER SIX

BASIC COMPUTER TERMS. __

Bit - A binary unit of data storage that can only be a value of 0 or 1.

BIOS - BIOS stands for Basic Input/Output System and it is a low level program used by your system to interface to computer devices such as your video card, keyboard, mouse, hard drive, and other devices.

Boot - A term used to describe what happens to a computer when it is turned on, the operating system begins to run, and then the user is able to use the computer successfully.

Byte - 8 bits of data which has a possible value from 0 to 255.

CD-ROM disk - A disk with about 640Mb of storage capacity which are more commonly read than written to.

CD-ROM drive - The hardware component that is used to read a CD-ROM or write to it. Crash - A common term used to describe what happens to a computer when software errors force it to quit operating and become unresponsive to a computer user.

Driver - A specially written program which understands the operation of the device it interfaces to, such as a printer, video card, sound card or CD ROM drive. It provides an interface for the operating system to use the device. File - A collection of data into a permanent storage structure. Stored on a permanent storage media such as a computer hard drive. Firmware - Software written into permanent storage into the computer.

Floppy disk - A low capacity storage media which can be written to as easily as it is read. Floppy Drive - The hardware component that is used to read or write to a floppy disk. Hardware - Describes the physical parts of your computer which you can physically touch or see such as your monitor, case, disk drives, microprocessor and other physical parts. Internet - A network of networks which incorporate a many organizations, physical lines, the ability to route data, and many services including email and web browsing. ISP - Internet Service Provider is an organization

that provides the ability to connect to the internet for their customers. They also usually provide additional services such as e-mail and the ability to host web sites.

MIME - multipurpose internet mail extension Memory - Used to provide the temporary storage of information function.

Network - A general term describing to the cables and electronic components that carry data between computers. It is also generally used to refer to the server computers that provide services such as printing, file sharing, e-mail, and other services.

Operating System - The core software component of a computer providing the ability to interface to peripheral and external devices along with program functions to support appllication programs.

Parallel - A data transmission method where data is sent on more than one line at a time. This may be any number of bits at a time, but is usually one word at a time (two bytes) or possibly three bytes at a time.

Protocols - A standard method used for communications or other internet and network functions.

Security flaw - A software bug allowing an attacker a method to gain anauthorized access to a system. Serial - A data transmission method where data is sent on a single line and one bit is sent at at a time. This is similar to a line which one item must come one after another Software - Describes the programs that run on your system.

SPAM - A term used to describe junk and unsolicited e-mail.

Storage Media - A term used to describe any magnetic device that computer data can be permanently stored on such as a hard drive or floppy drive.

URL - Uniform Resource Locator is the term used to describe a link which points to a location of a file on the internet.

Virus - A program that runs on a system against the owner's or user's wishes and knowledge and can spread by infecting files or sending itself

through e-mail

Vulnerability - Software errors that allow some kind of unauthorized access when they are used or exploited.

Word - Two bytes or 16 bits of data with a possible unsigned value from 0 to 16535.

Worm - A term used to describe an unwanted program that uses system or application vulnerabilities to infect a computer without the user doing anything but connecting to an infected network.

RUNNING THE WINDOWS BUILT IN
DIAGNOSTIC TOOL.

Hold down the Windows key and press the "X"
key on the keyboard to get to the RUN window

Type in the RUN window, DXDIAG and click
OK

The Windows Diagnostics will be displayed,
and will begin the internal Diagnostics; follow the
instructions.

TEST YOUR NETWORK CARD.____

Use the command " PING " to perform a Loopback
Test to check the Network Adapter on the
Computer.

Use the command: PING

To test Network Card with Loopback Test.

Type CMD, and from the CMD Window type:
Ping 127.0.0.1

WHAT IS PING UTILITY IN WINDOWS. ____

Ping sends 32 bytes of data to the address 127.0.0.1 which is the default IP address of the Network Adapter Card. This data is then loopback to the sender to complete the tests send/receive with no errors. If errors are detected then the Network Adapter could be defective.

CHAPTER SEVEN

Your Computer Hardware Ports and your Desktop.

Most computers will have the following standard hardware ports; a printer port, the CD/DVD port, the mouse and keyboard ports, the microphone and audio ports, at least three to four USB ports, the video port, the Ethernet port, the power input port. The USB ports will serve as external ports to connect multiple devices, such as an external Hard Drive or external camera or Webcam.

Your computer hardware ports have *designated hardware symbols* to identify each port. A list of these hardware symbols are contained in this book. Each symbol is imprinted on the external hardware case to identify the port. These symbols meet international standards for hardware identification ports and some have become " *defacto standards.* "

Your Desktop. _____

Your Desktop is one of the most important parts of your computer. When you turn on your computer it will boot up and display your desktop window. Your desktop will have a background color or image that can be changed by the user. Your desktop can get corrupted and it is very important to keep your desktop clean from clutter. Having many icons on your desktop will create clutter and take up storage space.

Protected Folders on your Computer._____

Special folders were created to keep your user documents and personal files, in order to keep them organized and off your desktop.

Such folders that are protected are: The *Documents folder*, the *Music folder*, the *Pictures folder*, and the *Videos folder*.

Some icons are required to be on your desktop so that they can be accessible immediately by the user and the system, such as: *My Computer, My Network* and *Internet Explorer* or IE.

If you need to put a copy of documents, pictures or other files you use daily, then you should put them into folders, if they are going to reside on your desktop; and not leave the icon open on your desktop. You could also create " *shortcuts* " of your documents and or applications or any other files you wish to leave on your desktop, instead of leaving the original document or image.

Shortcuts do not take up a lot of space or memory. Your desktop icons can be changed in the Control Panel in " *Personalization.* "

Laptop computers vs. Desktop computers vs. Notebook computers. ___

Laptop computers were designed to be mobile, containing a battery that would provide from two to four hours of continuing use, and provide all the software and connections necessary to allow the user to work in a wireless environment. Laptops are now fabricated with great processor speeds and large amounts of memory and storage. Desktop computers are the more traditional form of computers built to be fixed in a home or office environment containing very large boxes with many drives and devices. These hardware boxes are generally heavy and are called " *chassis*" and they contain very large power supplies and storage drives that are heavy.

Notebook computers are usually very light and just have a basic operating system designed to provide the most minimum capabilities and connections. They are also limited in processor speed, memory and storage capability. Some notebook computers are now been built with similar capabilities like laptops, with very fast processors. The most popular laptops and notebooks are made by HP (Hewlett Packard), Toshiba, Samsung, and others.

The Task Manager.__

Since computers are Task driven machines, and operate by tasks and processes, a Task Manager was built into the OS to manage and organize computer tasks for the user. Sometimes the user will overload the computer with multiple tasks at the same time, and the computer will freeze or crash as it runs out of memory trying to perform all of the tasks requested by the user. Sometimes the users will assume that computers are multitasking machines and they forget that to do multi-tasking, any computer must meet the following minimum criteria:

- 📂🖱 Must have large amounts of memory (8, 16, or 32 GB)

- 📄🖱 A very fast processor (Intel dual-core I-5 I-7 , I-9 or higher)

- 📄🖱 A large storage area (1 TB to 1.5 TB) Hard Drive

The Task Manager will also allow killing a process that hangs causing the computer to freeze, and also allowing the user that is logged on, to " disconnect himself" from the computer without login off.

You can access the Task Manager two ways: From the keyboard, press down at the same time, CTRL+ALT+DEL keys,

And also with the CTRL+SHIFT+ESC Keys.

The Task Manager will also show applications that are running, all of the Background processes as well as all of the Windows processes.

It will also show all of the applications that have an impact when your computer startup, and the services that are running in Windows.

The Antivirus Software Program on your Computer._

All computers must have at least a basic Antivirus software program installed on the computer to provide protection against Viruses. Beware of Security programs that are available and claim to protect your computer from viruses, to protect your computer from viruses, you will need to have a full paid version or a basic Free version installed and configured on your computer. The Antivirus Software program should Scan your computer after it has been installed, your computer must be connected to the internet only to get the Virus Definition File Update. The Virus Definition File updates your Antivirus program software, so that any known viruses or late published threats, will be known by your Antivirus program, before you run a Scan. Normally after the installation is done your Antivirus program will automatically connect via the internet and update its Definition file before running a Scan.

Once your Antivirus is updated, the next time you run a Scan on your computer; you must be disconnected from the Internet. to disconnect you may turn off your Router or Disable your Ethernet and or Wireless Network Adapters in the Control Panel. Once the scan is completed and no viruses are found, you can re-connect your computer to the Internet or turn back on your Router and or Network Adapter cards.

Run your Antivirus program at least once a week. And keep your Virus Definition File up to date.

Many Antivirus programs exist; the most popular paid versions are made by: Norton, MacAfee, Panda and others.

The Free basic Antivirus that is very popular is made by AVG. It is called AVG Antivirus and is recommended.

AVG Antivirus can be downloaded from the Internet for free as well as others.

Both the Free versions and the paid versions will provide the protection you need. Do not connect your computer to the Internet if you do not have an Antivirus program installed on your machine. Beware of Trialware Antivirus programs that come with your computer, since they will expire in 30 to 45 days and do not offer any protection to your computer, since they are not a full version of the original software and do not contain all of the software modules. Most of them have no Virus Definition files to update.

When Antivirus Programs do not work. __

Most Antivirus programs will not work if their Virus Definition File (VDF) is not up to date.

About Computers. __

We human users are different from Machines (Computer Hardware) in many ways.

 To find the Solution to a problem we can use our brains in various ways:

We use CRITICAL THINKING

LOGICAL THINKING

CONDITIONAL THINKING

COMPARATIVE THINKING

ANALYTICAL THINKING

STATISTICAL THINKING

At the same time.

Which gives us "Reasoning ".

Machines, use " ANALITICAL Thinking" , based on TASKs as

Computers are TASK DRIVEN Machines.

We must realize sometimes that we are asking a "Machine" to give us information that we want, not realizing that machines do not "Think like us" and they have Hardware Limitations.

We must never try to tell a machine " Computer" How to do its Job. As most machines operate under the Protocol "H" and humans use Protocol "W".

Protocol " H" is the " How to do" Protocol;

How to complete the task I have been given

How to connect the Cables

How to interface correctly with the user

How to process the information my user needs

How to use my memory efficiently

How to turn on my machine

How to Display my Desktop

How to protect the machine from Viruses and other malware.

Protocol "W" is the WHAT, WHEN, WHERE, WHY, WHO, WITH, WHICH, of what Computers should do.

Where do I go to get the information, I am looking for.?

What do I do if my Computer "FREEZES" or get the "BLUE SCREEN OF DEATH"?

What Utilities are available to me to Resolve my problem.

Why is my Application not working.?

When can I access my Data.?

Who loaded this Application or Utility.? The System or the User.?

Which Browser should I use.?

With all the Tasks I am asking my Computer to do, will it work ok and correctly.?

Sometimes we are looking for Information in the wrong places, and assume that Computers can and will go to the correct place to find the information for us, (A Human Response); we forget the Limitations and did not give the Machine a clear Task to do. (we assume that the Computer knows where to go to find the information even tough, we did not give it the correct Task, a WHERE to go, a WHAT we are looking for.

Sometimes we need to THINK like Machines. Analytical Thinking. To convey to the Machine

WHAT we want. Our request will always be converted to Zero's and One's; the Machine Language.

When we are looking for information on the INTERNET and we use a Computer with the necessary Software, we need to go to the correct Places on the INTERNET so that the Computer SOFTWARE can work to find the information we are looking for.

Then the Question is; WHERE do we go.

INTERNET DEFINITIONS. _

Internet

An international conglomeration of interconnected computer networks. Begun in the late 1960s, it was developed in the 1970s to allow government and university researchers to share information. The Internet is not controlled by any single group or organization. Its original focus was research and communications, but it continues to expand, offering a wide array of resources for business and home users.

IP (Internet Protocol) address

An Internet Protocol address is a unique set of numbers used to locate another computer on a network. The format of an IP address is a 32bit string of four numbers separated by periods. Each number can be from 0 to 255 (i.e., 1.154.10.255). Within a closed network IP addresses may be assigned at random, however, IP addresses of Web Servers must be registered to avoid duplicates.

The Purpose of Creating a Restore Point in Windows.

It is so important to create a Restore Point in Windows to avoid loosing all of your work. And many times the Computer might freeze up caused by a virus or some other problem, and the user may not be able to get to his files or access Windows.

Restoring all of the user files from a " Known good date" is critical and will save the day.

Follow the instructions on the next page to setup and create a RESTORE POINT.

Enable System Protection / Create a Restore Point

What happens if you install a bad piece of software or a defective driver and your computer starts acting strangely or you can't even boot. You'll want to revert Windows 10 to the previous system restore point, which will turn back the clock on your drivers, programs and settings to a time when the system worked perfectly. However, Windows 10 comes with system protection disabled. If you want to protect yourself -- and you should -- set up restore points following the instructions below.

1. Search for "restore point" in the Windows search box.

2. Launch "Create a restore point" from the results. You should see a list of available drives.

3. Select the system drive and click Configure.

The system drive is usually the C: drive and has the word "(System)" written after its volume name.

4. Toggle Restore Settings to "Turn on system protection," set the maximum disk space usage by moving the slider and click Ok. We recommend leaving 2 or 3 percent for restore pints but you may be able to get away with the lowest (1 percent).

5. Click Create so that you create an initial restore point right away.

6. Name the   initial   restore   point when prompted.

7. Click Close when it is done.

If you need to restore from one of these points, you can click the System Restore button on the System Protection tab. If you can't boot, you can hit F8 or Shift + F8 during boot to get to the emergency menu on some computers. On other PCs, if you can at least get to the log in screen, you can hold down Shift while you select Restart.

CHAPTER EIGHT

WINDOWS SHORTCUTS. ___

1. Press and Hold the Windows Key, then press "T" to access all Pinned Applications on bottom toolbar.

2. Press and hold the Windows Key (WinKey) and press R to Open the RUN Dialog.

3. Shift + F8 to access " SAFE MODE " when Computer is booting up

4. Open RUN Dialog and type : Shell:AppsFolder to access the " All Applications Folder" ..

5. Slide to Shutdown Windows Utility, located in C:/Windows/system32 on the Hard Drive

Windows System Key combinations.__

- ☐ F1: Help
- ☐ CTRL+ESC: Open Start menu
- ☐ ALT+TAB: Switch between open programs
- ☐ ALT+F4: Quit program
- ☐ SHIFT+DELETE: Delete item permanently

- ☐ Windows (WinKey) Logo+L: Lock the computer (without using CTRL+ALT+DELETE)

Windows program key combinations

- ☐ CTRL+C: Copy
- ☐ CTRL+X: Cut
- ☐ CTRL+V: Paste
- ☐ CTRL+Z: Undo
- ☐ CTRL+B: Bold
- ☐ CTRL+U: Underline

- ☐ CTRL+I: Italic

Mouse click/keyboard modifier combinations for shell objects

- ☐ SHIFT+right click: Displays a shortcut menu containing alternative commands
- ☐ SHIFT+double click: Runs the alternate default command (the second item on the menu)

◻ ALT+double click: Displays properties

◻ SHIFT+DELETE: Deletes an item immediately without placing it in the Recycle Bin

General keyboard-only commands

◻ F1: Starts Windows Help

◻ F10: Activates menu bar options

◻ SHIFT+F10 Opens a shortcut menu for the selected item (this is the same as right-clicking an object

◻ <u>CTRL+ESC: Opens the Start menu</u> (use the ARROW keys to select an item)

◻ CTRL+ESC or ESC: Selects the Start button (press TAB to select the taskbar, or press SHIFT+F10 for a context menu)

◻ <u>CTRL+SHIFT+ESC: Opens Windows Task Manager</u>

◻ ALT+DOWN ARROW: Opens a drop-down list box

◻ ALT+TAB: Switch to another running program (hold down the ALT key and then press the TAB key to view the task-switching window)

- SHIFT: Press and hold down the SHIFT key while you insert a CD-ROM to bypass the automatic-run feature
- ALT+SPACE: Displays the main window's System menu (from the System menu, you can restore, move, resize, minimize, maximize, or close the window)
- ALT+- (ALT+hyphen): Displays the Multiple Document Interface (MDI) child window's System menu (from the MDI child window's System menu, you can restore, move, resize, minimize, maximize, or close the child window)
- CTRL+TAB: Switch to the next child window of a Multiple Document Interface (MDI) program
- ALT+underlined letter in menu: Opens the menu
- ALT+F4: Closes the current window
- CTRL+F4: Closes the current Multiple Document Interface (MDI) window

- ALT+F6: Switch between multiple windows in the same program (for example, when the Notepad Find dialog box is displayed,

  ALT+F6 switches between the Find dialog box and the main Notepad window)

Shell objects and general folder/Windows Explorer shortcuts

For a selected object:

- ☐ F2: Rename object
- ☐ F3: Find all files
- ☐ CTRL+X: Cut
- ☐ CTRL+C: Copy
- ☐ CTRL+V: Paste
- ☐ <u>SHIFT+DELETE: Delete selection immediately,</u> without moving the item to the Recycle Bin

- ☐ ALT+ENTER: Open the properties for the selected object

To copy a file

Press and hold down the CTRL key while you drag the file to another folder.

To create a shortcut

<u>Press and hold down CTRL+SHIFT while you drag a file to the desktop or a folder.</u>

General folder/shortcut control

- F4: Selects the Go To A Different Folder box and moves down the entries in the box (if the toolbar is active in Windows Explorer) ⬚ F5: Refreshes the current window.
- F6: Moves among panes in Windows Explorer
- CTRL+G: Opens the Go To Folder tool (in Windows 95 Windows Explorer only)
- CTRL+Z: Undo the last command
- CTRL+A: Select all the items in the current window
- BACKSPACE: Switch to the parent folder

- SHIFT+click+Close button: For folders, close the current folder plus all parent folders

Windows Explorer tree control

- Numeric Keypad *: Expands everything under the current selection
- Numeric Keypad +: Expands the current selection
- Numeric Keypad -: Collapses the current selection.

- RIGHT ARROW: Expands the current

selection if it is not expanded, otherwise goes to the first child

☐ LEFT ARROW: Collapses the current selection if it is expanded, otherwise goes to the parent

Properties control

☐ CTRL+TAB/CTRL+SHIFT+TAB: Move through the property tabs

Accessibility shortcuts

☐ Press SHIFT five times: Toggles StickyKeys on and off
☐ Press down and hold the right SHIFT key for eight seconds: Toggles FilterKeys on and off
☐ Press down and hold the NUM LOCK key for five seconds: Toggles ToggleKeys on and off
☐ Left ALT+left SHIFT+NUM LOCK: Toggles MouseKeys on and off

☐ Left ALT+left SHIFT+PRINT SCREEN: Toggles high contrast on and off

Microsoft Natural Keyboard keys

☐ Windows Logo: Start menu

- Windows Logo+R: <u>Run dialog box</u>
- Windows Logo+M: Minimize all
- SHIFT+Windows Logo+M: Undo minimize all
- Windows Logo+F1: Help
- Windows Logo+E: Windows Explorer
- Windows Logo+F: Find files or folders
- Windows Logo+D: Minimizes all open windows and displays the desktop
- CTRL+Windows Logo+F: Find computer
- CTRL+Windows Logo+TAB: Moves focus from Start, to the Quick Launch toolbar, to the system tray (use RIGHT ARROW or LEFT ARROW to move focus to items on the Quick Launch toolbar and the system tray)
- Windows Logo+TAB: Cycle through taskbar buttons
- Windows Logo+Break: System Properties dialog box

- Application key: Displays a shortcut menu for the selected item

Microsoft Natural Keyboard with IntelliType software installed

- Windows Logo+L: Log off Windows

- [] Windows Logo+P: Starts Print Manager
- [] Windows Logo+C: Opens Control Panel
- [] Windows Logo+V: Starts Clipboard
- [] Windows Logo+K: Opens Keyboard Properties dialog box
- [] Windows Logo+I: Opens Mouse Properties dialog box
- [] Windows Logo+A: Starts Accessibility Options (if installed)
- [] Windows Logo+SPACEBAR: Displays the list of Microsoft IntelliType shortcut keys

- [] Windows Logo+S: Toggles CAPS LOCK on and off

Dialog box keyboard commands

- [] TAB: Move to the next control in the dialog box
- [] SHIFT+TAB: Move to the previous control in the dialog box
- [] SPACEBAR: If the current control is a button, this clicks the button. If the current control is a check box, this toggles the check box. If the current control is an option, this selects the option.

◻ ENTER: Equivalent to clicking the selected button (the button with the outline) ◻ ESC: Equivalent to clicking the Cancel button

◻ ALT+underlined letter in dialog box item: Move to the corresponding item

Windows Security Setup. ___

A Graphic View.

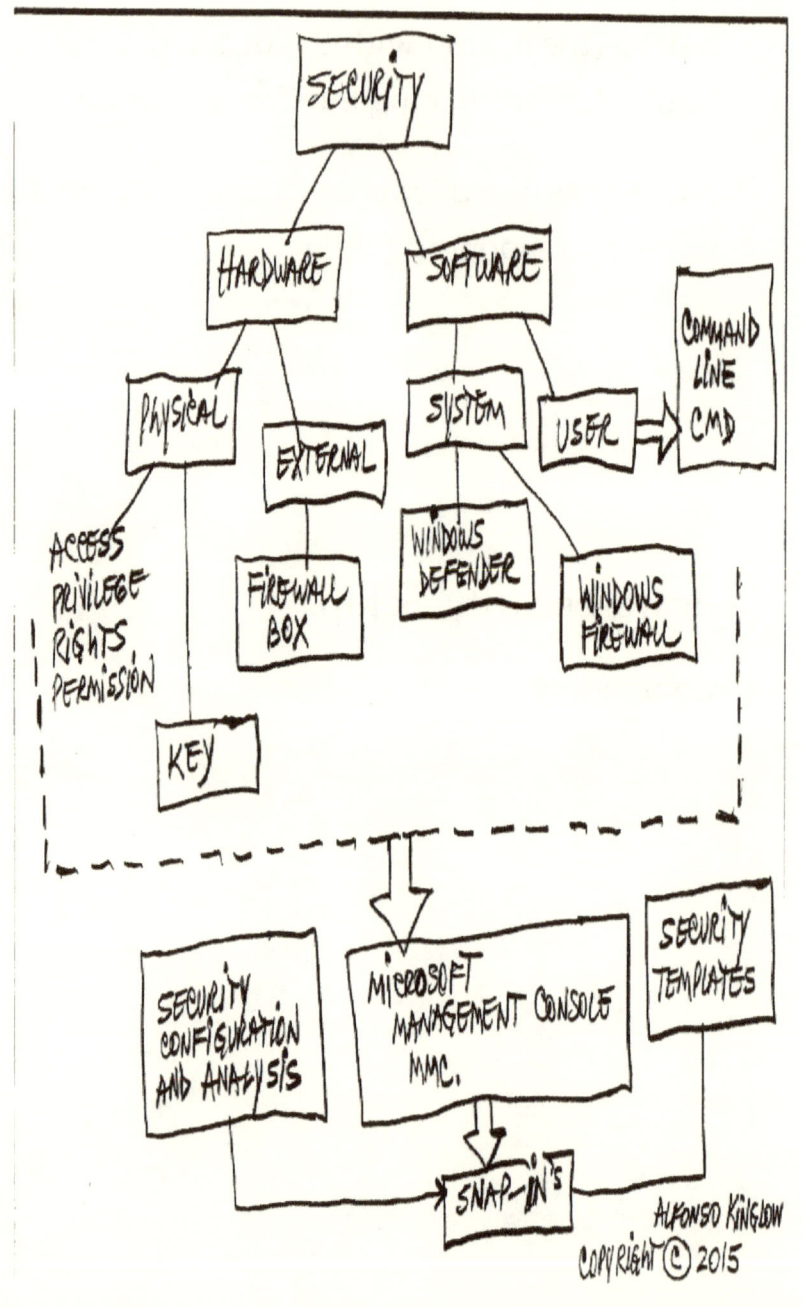

NOTES

CHAPTER NINE

(MMC) Microsoft Management Console. __

 MMC is a Microsoft Built In Utility to Manage the user computer, allowing the users to create " SNAPINS " to manage specific parts of the Windows HARDWARE and SOFTWARE.

Step-by-Step Guide to the Microsoft Management Console

The Microsoft Management Console (MMC) lets system administrators and Users create much more flexible user interfaces and customize administration tools. This step-bystep guide explores some of these new features.

Introduction

MMC unifies and simplifies day-to-day system management tasks. It hosts tools and displays them as consoles. These tools, consisting of one or more applications, are built with modules called snap-ins. The snapins also can include additional extension snap-ins. MMC is a core part of Microsoft's management strategy and is included in Microsoft Windows® operating systems. In addition, Microsoft development groups will use MMC for future management applications.

Microsoft Management Console enables system administrators to create special tools to delegate specific administrative tasks to users or groups. Microsoft provides standard tools with the operating system that perform everyday administrative tasks that users need to accomplish. These are part of the All Users profile of the computer and located in the Administrative Tools group on the Startup menu. Saved as MMC console (.msc) files, these custom tools can be sent by e-mail, shared in a network folder, or posted on the Web. They can also be assigned to users, groups, or computers with system policy settings. A tool can be scaled up and down, integrated seamlessly into the operating system, repackaged, and customized.

Using MMC, system administrators can create unique consoles for workers who report to them or for workgroup managers. They can assign a tool with a system policy, deliver the file by e-mail, or post the file to a shared location on the network. When a workgroup manager opens the .msc file, access will be restricted to those tools provided by the system administrator.

Building your own tools with the standard user interface in MMC is a straightforward process. Start with an existing console and modify or add components to fulfill your needs. Or create an entirely new console. The following example shows how to create a new console and arrange its administrative components into separate windows.

Prerequisites and Requirements

There are no prerequisites: you don't need to complete any other step-by-step guide before starting this guide. You need one computer running either Windows Professional or Windows Server. For the most current information about hardware requirements and compatibility for servers, clients, and peripherals, see the Check Hardware and Software Compatibility page on the Windows website.

Creating Consoles

The most common way for administrators to use MMC is to simply start a predefined console file from the Start menu. However, to get an idea of the flexibility of MMC, it is useful to create a console file from scratch. It is also useful to create a console file from scratch when using the new task delegation features in this version of MMC.

Creating a New Console File

12.   On the Start Menu, click Run, type MMC, and then click OK. Microsoft Management Console opens with an empty console (or administrative tool) as shown in Figure 1 below. The empty console has no management functionality until you add some snap-ins. The MMC menu commands on the menu bar at the top of the Microsoft Management Console window apply to the entire console.

Figure 1: Beginning Console Window

13.   Click Console (under Console1). On the Console Menu, click Add/Remove Snap-in. The Add/Remove Snap-in dialog box opens. This lets you enable extensions and configure which snap-ins are in the console file. You can specify

where the snap-ins should be inserted in the Snap-in's "added to drop-down box." Accept the default, Console Root, for this exercise.

Click Add. This displays the Add Standalone Snap-in dialog box that lists the snap-ins that are installed on your computer.

From the list of snap-ins, double-click Computer Management to open the Computer Management wizard.

Click Local computer and select the check box for "Allow the selected computer to be changed when launching from the command line."

Click Finish. This returns you to the Add/Remove Snap-ins dialog box. Click Close.

Click the Extensions tab as shown in Figure 2 below. By selecting the check box Add all extensions, all locally-installed extensions on the computer are used. If this check box is not selected, then any extension snap-in that is selected is explicitly loaded when the console file is opened on a different computer.

Figure 2: Select All Extensions

Click OK to close the Add/Remove Snap-in dialog box. The Console Root window now has a snap-in, Computer Management, rooted at the Console Root folder.

Customizing the Display of Snap-ins in the Console:
New Windows

After you add the snap-ins, you can add windows to provide different administrative views in the console. To add windows

In the left pane of the tree view in Figure 3 below, click the + next to Computer Management. Click System Tools.

Figure 3: Console1: System Tools

Right-click the Event Viewer folder that opens, and
then click New window from here. As shown
in Figure 4 below, this opens a new
Event Viewer window rooted at the Event
Viewer extension to computer management.

Figure 4: Event Viewer

Click Window and click Console Root.

In the Console Root window, click
Services and Applications, right-click Services in
the left pane, and then click New Window. As
shown in Figure 5 below, this opens a new
Services window rooted at the Event Viewer
extension to Computer Management. In the
new window, click the Show/Hide Console
Tree toolbar button to hide the console tree, as
shown in the red circle in Figure 5 below.

Figure 5: Show/Hide Button

Close the original window with Console Root

showing in it.

On the Window menu, select Tile
Horizontally. The console file should appear and
include the information shown in Figure 4 and
Figure 5 above.

You can now save your new MMC
console. Click the Save as icon on the Console
window, and give your console a name. Your
console is now saved as a .msc file, and you
can provide it to anyone who needs to
configure a computer with these tools.

Note: Each of the two smaller windows has a
toolbar with buttons and drop-down menus.
The toolbar buttons and drop-down menus on
these each of these two windows apply only to
the contents of the window. You can see that a
window's toolbar buttons and menus change
depending on the snap-in selected in the left
pane of the window. If you select the View
menu, you can see a list of available toolbars.

Tip: The windows fit better if your monitor display
is set to a higher resolution and small font.

Creating Console Taskpads

If you are creating a console file for another
user, it's useful to provide a very simplified
view with only a few tasks available.
Console taskpads help you to do this.

To create a console Taskpad

From the Window menu, select New Window.
Close the other two windows (you will save a
new console file at the end of this procedure).
Maximize the remaining window.

In the left pane, click the + next to the
Computer Management folder, then click the
+ next to the System Tools folder. Click
System, click the Event Viewer folder,
rightclick System, and select New Taskpad
View.

Go through the wizard accepting all the
default settings. Verify the checkbox on the
last page is checked so that the Task Creation
wizard can start automatically.

Choose the defaults in the Task Creation wizard until you come to the page shown below in Figure 6, then choose a list view task and select Properties:

Figure 6: New Task Wizard

Click Next and accept the defaults for the rest of the screens. By selecting an Event and clicking Properties, you can see the property page for that Event.

After you click Finish on the last screen, your console should look like Figure 7 below:

Figure 7: New Console Showing System Event Log

Click the Show/Hide console tree toolbar button.

From the view menu, click Customize and click each of the options except the Description bar to hide each type of toolbar.

The next section discusses how to lock the console file down so that the user sees only a limited view. For right now your console file should look like Figure 8 below.

Figure 8: Customized View

Setting Console File Options

If you are creating a console file for another user, it is useful to prevent that user from further customizing the console file. The Options dialog box allows you to do this.

To set console file options

From the Console menu, select Options.

Change the Console Mode by selecting User Modelimited access, single window from the drop-down dialog box. This will prevent a user from adding new snap-ins to the console file or rearranging the windows.

You can change the name from Console1. Click
OK to continue.

Save the console file. The changes will not take
effect until the console file is opened again.

This is just one example of how the Microsoft
Management Console lets you group
information and functionality that previously
would have required opening a Control
Panel option plus two separate
administrative tools. The modular
architecture of MMC makes it easy for
system network developers to create snap-in
applications that leverage the platform while
easing administrative load.

NOTES

CHAPTER TEN

A Graphic View of different parts and aspect of Windows Software and Hardware. ____

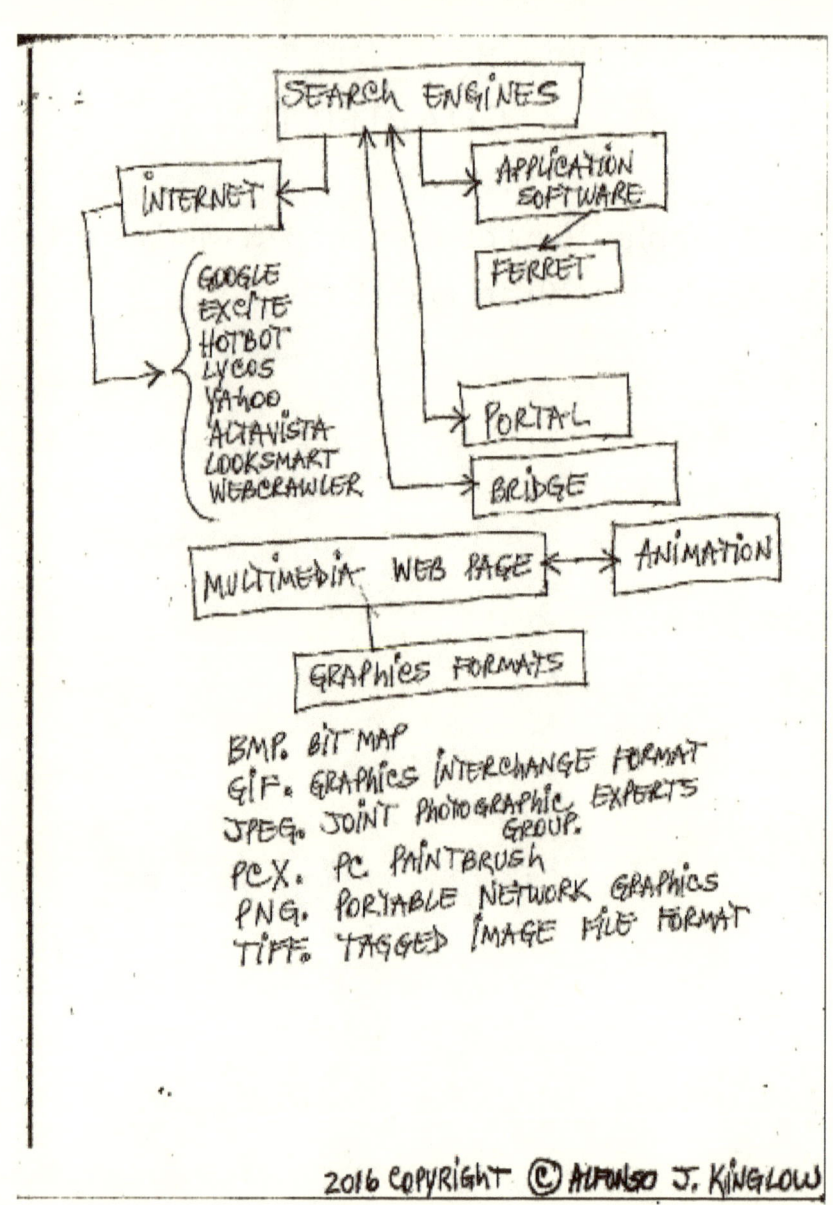

SEARCH ENGINES

INTERNET

APPLICATION SOFTWARE

FERRET

GOOGLE
EXCITE
HOTBOT
LYCOS
YAHOO
ALTAVISTA
LOOKSMART
WEBCRAWLER

PORTAL

BRIDGE

MULTIMEDIA WEB PAGE

ANIMATION

GRAPHICS FORMATS

BMP. BIT MAP
GIF. GRAPHICS INTERCHANGE FORMAT
JPEG. JOINT PHOTOGRAPHIC EXPERTS GROUP.
PCX. PC PAINTBRUSH
PNG. PORTABLE NETWORK GRAPHICS
TIFF. TAGGED IMAGE FILE FORMAT

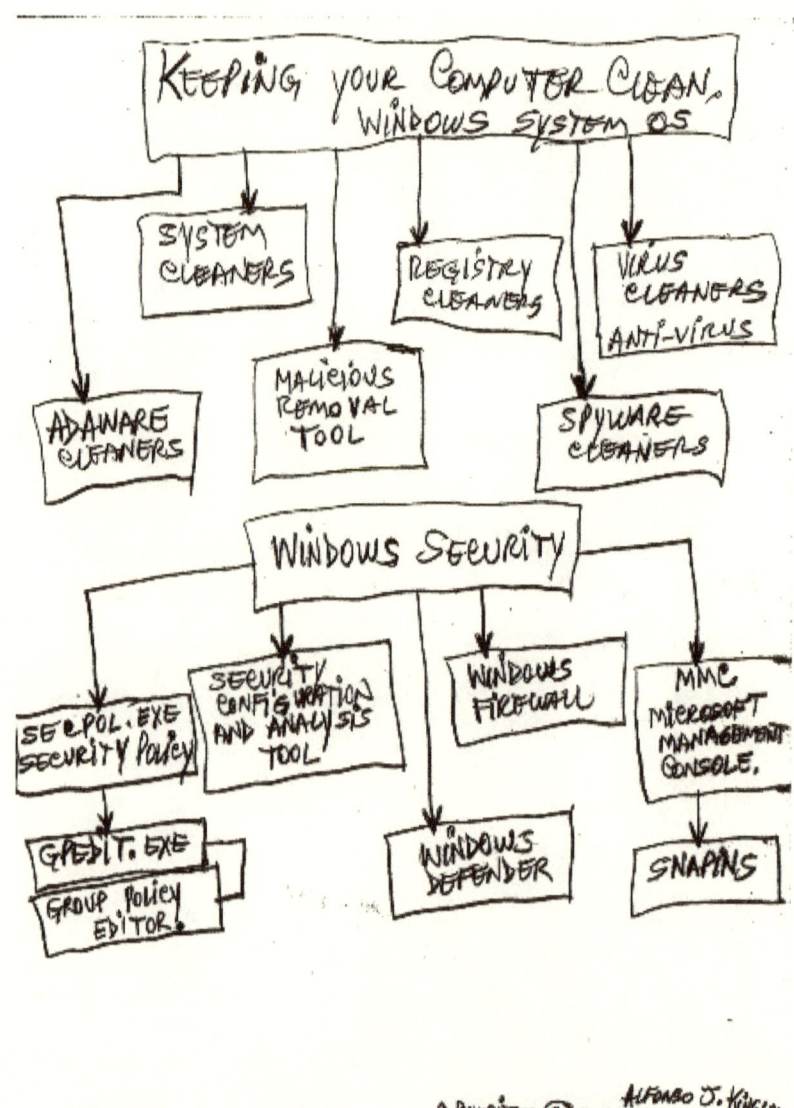

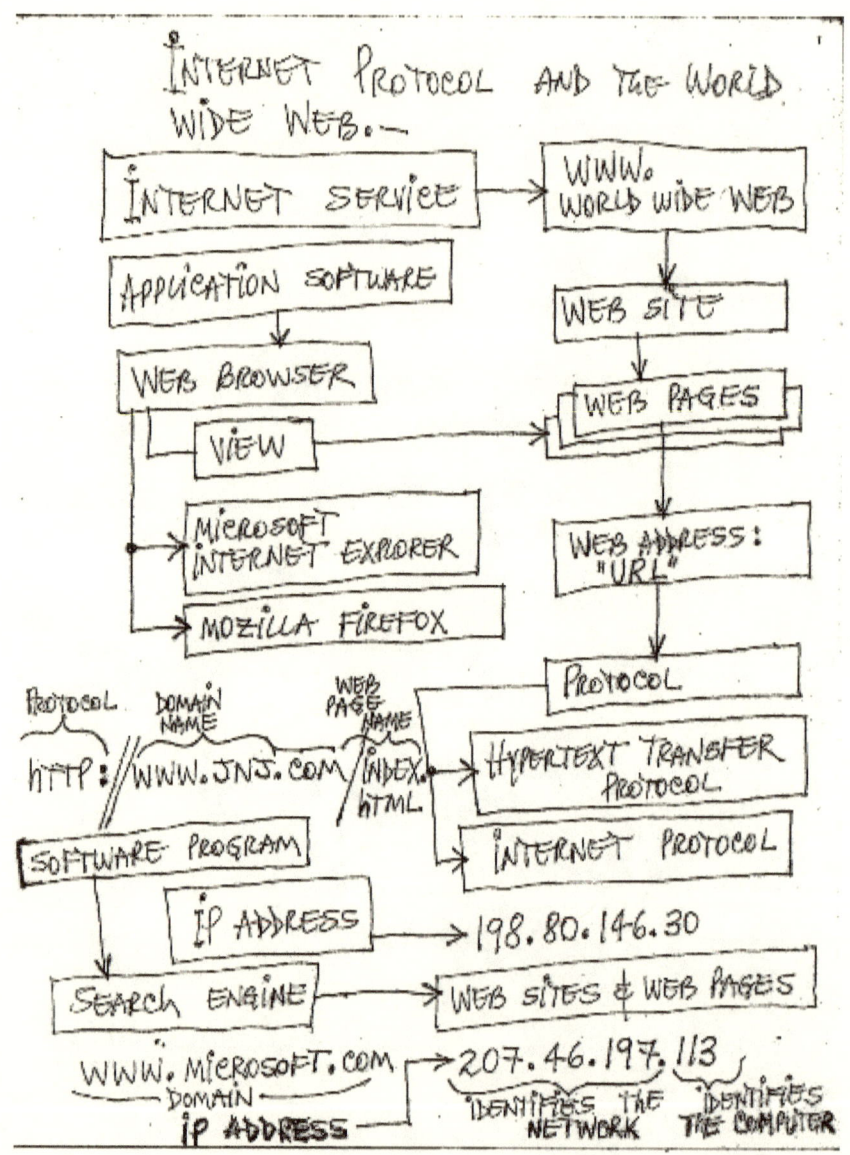

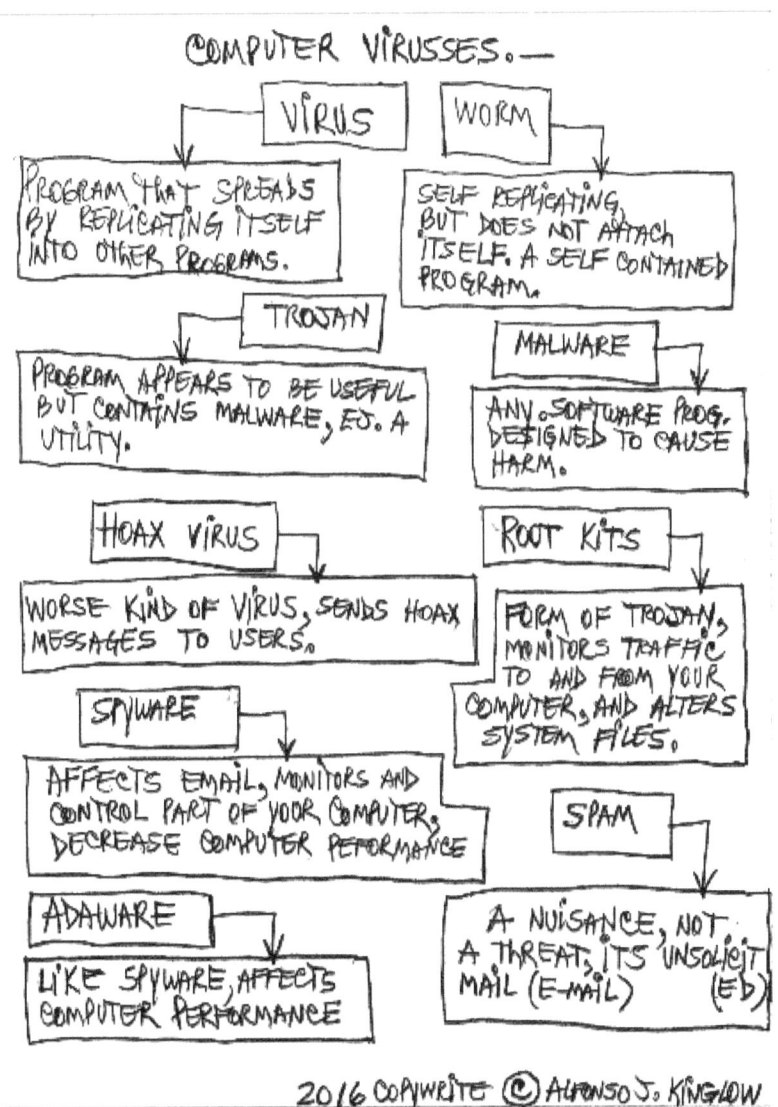

COMPUTER VIRUSSES.—

VIRUS

PROGRAM THAT SPREADS BY REPLICATING ITSELF INTO OTHER PROGRAMS.

WORM

SELF REPLICATING, BUT DOES NOT ATTACH ITSELF. A SELF CONTAINED PROGRAM.

TROJAN

PROGRAM APPEARS TO BE USEFUL BUT CONTAINS MALWARE, EJ. A UTILITY.

MALWARE

ANY SOFTWARE PROG. DESIGNED TO CAUSE HARM.

HOAX VIRUS

WORSE KIND OF VIRUS, SENDS HOAX MESSAGES TO USERS.

ROOT KITS

FORM OF TROJAN, MONITORS TRAFFIC TO AND FROM YOUR COMPUTER, AND ALTERS SYSTEM FILES.

SPYWARE

AFFECTS EMAIL, MONITORS AND CONTROL PART OF YOUR COMPUTER, DECREASE COMPUTER PERFORMANCE

SPAM

ADAWARE

LIKE SPYWARE, AFFECTS COMPUTER PERFORMANCE

A NUISANCE, NOT A THREAT, ITS UNSOLICIT MAIL (E-MAIL)   (ED)

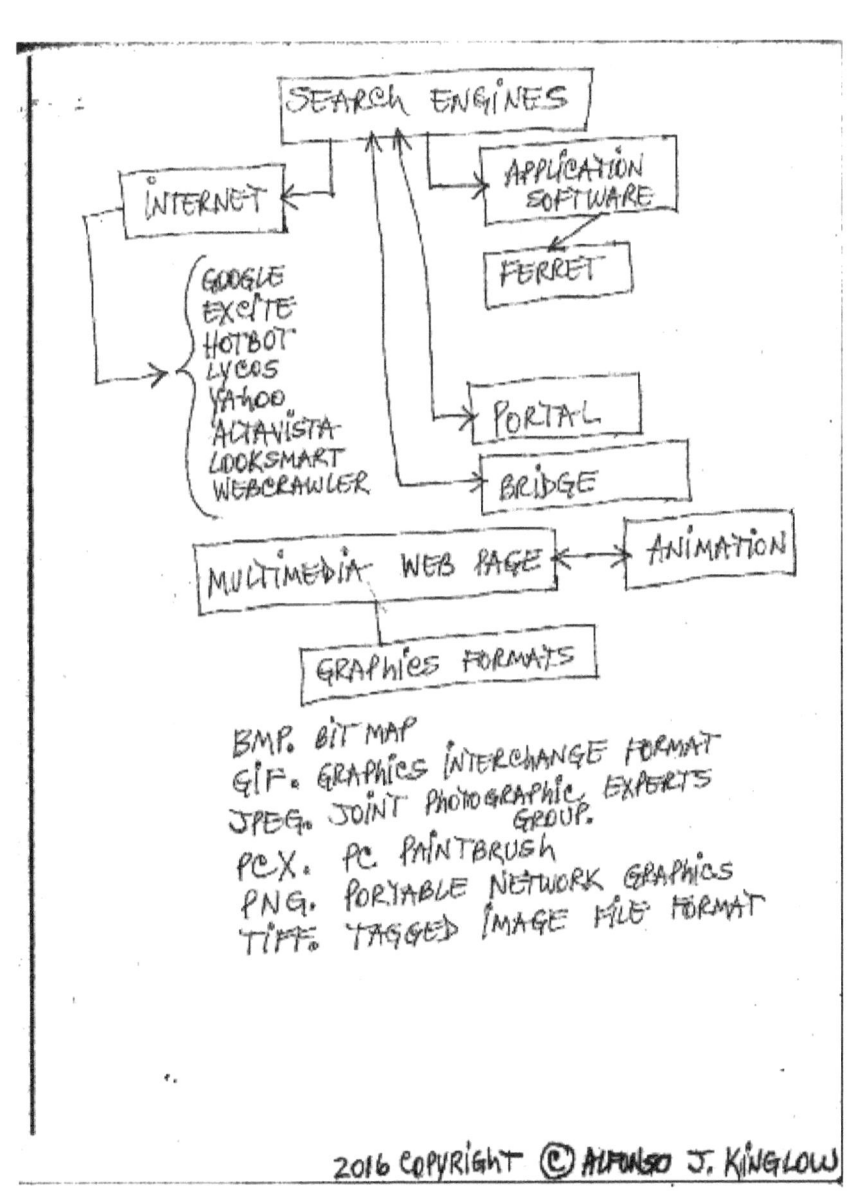

SEARCH ENGINES

INTERNET

APPLICATION SOFTWARE

FERRET

GOOGLE
EXCITE
HOTBOT
LYCOS
YAHOO
ALTAVISTA
LOOKSMART
WEBCRAWLER

PORTAL

BRIDGE

MULTIMEDIA WEB PAGE

ANIMATION

GRAPHICS FORMATS

BMP. BIT MAP
GIF. GRAPHICS INTERCHANGE FORMAT
JPEG. JOINT PHOTOGRAPHIC EXPERTS GROUP.
PCX. PC PAINTBRUSH
PNG. PORTABLE NETWORK GRAPHICS
TIFF. TAGGED IMAGE FILE FORMAT

2016 COPYRIGHT © ALFONSO J. KINGLOW

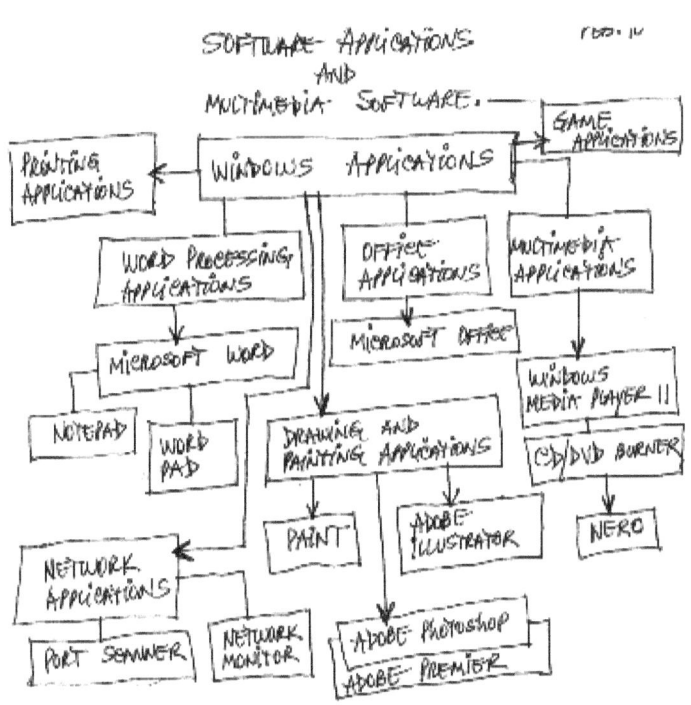

FIG. IV

SOFTWARE APPLICATIONS AND MULTIMEDIA SOFTWARE.

NOTE: INSTALL APPLICATIONS VS. RUN APPLICATIONS
UNINSTALL APPLICATIONS VS. DELETE APPLICATIONS
ADD AND REMOVE APPLICATIONS (SOFTWARE)
UTILITY VS. APPLICATIONS
USER INSTALL VS. SYSTEM INSTALL APPLICATIONS

DR ALFONSO J. KINGLOW

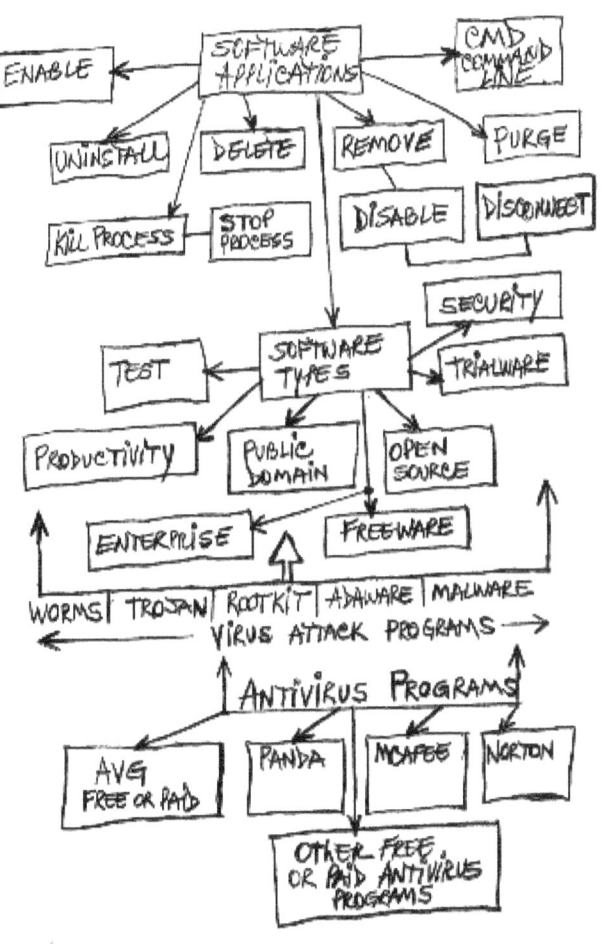

2016 COPYRIGHT ©ALFONSO J. KINGLOW

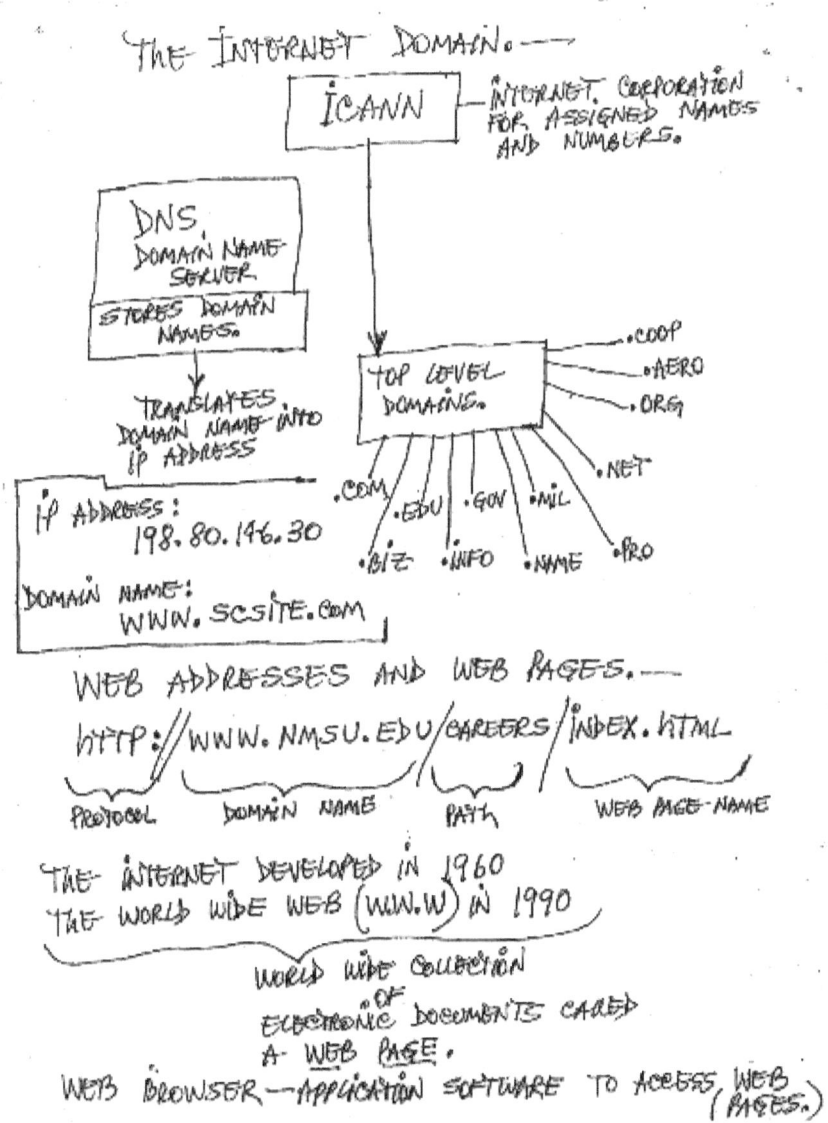

THE INTERNET DOMAIN.——

ICANN — INTERNET CORPORATION FOR ASSIGNED NAMES AND NUMBERS.

DNS.
DOMAIN NAME SERVER
STORES DOMAIN NAMES.

TRANSLATES DOMAIN NAME INTO IP ADDRESS

IP ADDRESS: 198.80.146.30

DOMAIN NAME: WWW. SCSITE.COM

TOP LEVEL DOMAINS.

.COOP
.AERO
.ORG
.NET
.COM .EDU .GOV .MIL
.BIZ .INFO .NAME .PRO

WEB ADDRESSES AND WEB PAGES.——

http://WWW.NMSU.EDU/CAREERS/INDEX.HTML

PROTOCOL   DOMAIN NAME   PATH   WEB PAGE NAME

THE INTERNET DEVELOPED IN 1960
THE WORLD WIDE WEB (WW.W) IN 1990

WORLD WIDE COLLECTION
OF ELECTRONIC DOCUMENTS CALLED A WEB PAGE.

WEB BROWSER — APPLICATION SOFTWARE TO ACCESS WEB (PAGES.)

DR ALFONSO J. KINGLOW

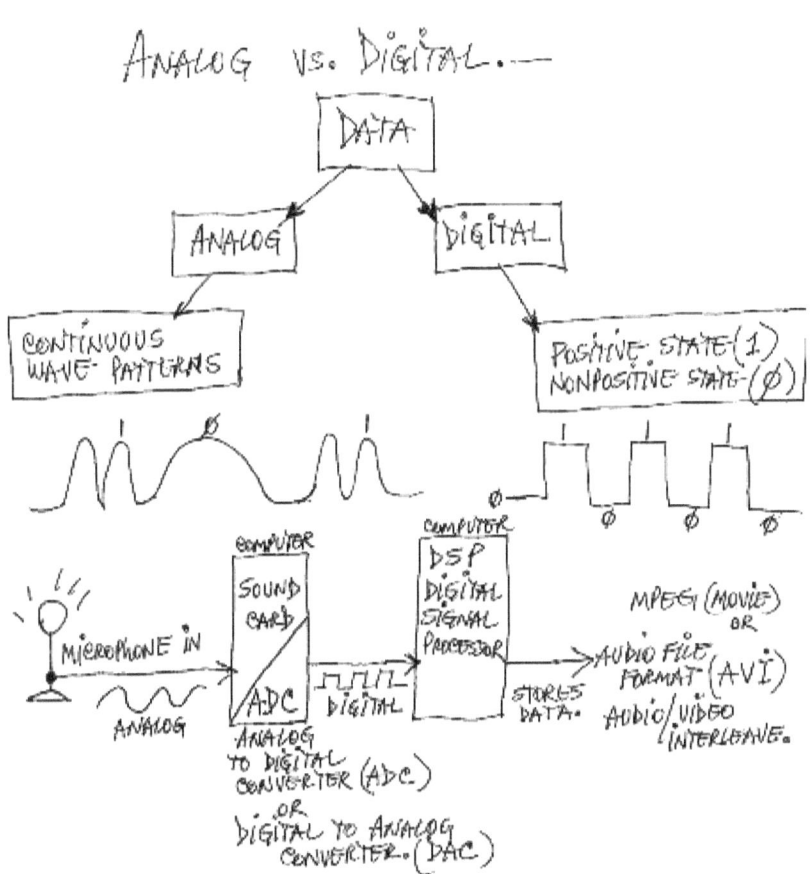

ANALOG vs. DIGITAL.—

DATA

ANALOG

DIGITAL

CONTINUOUS WAVE PATTERNS

POSITIVE STATE (1)
NONPOSITIVE STATE (∅)

COMPUTER
SOUND CARD
ADC
ANALOG TO DIGITAL CONVERTER (ADC.)
OR
DIGITAL TO ANALOG CONVERTER. (DAC.)

MICROPHONE IN
ANALOG
DIGITAL

COMPUTER
DSP
DIGITAL SIGNAL PROCESSOR

STORES DATA.

MPEG (MOVIE) OR
AUDIO FILE FORMAT. (AVI)
AUDIO/VIDEO INTERLEAVE.

DR ALFONSO J. KINGLOW

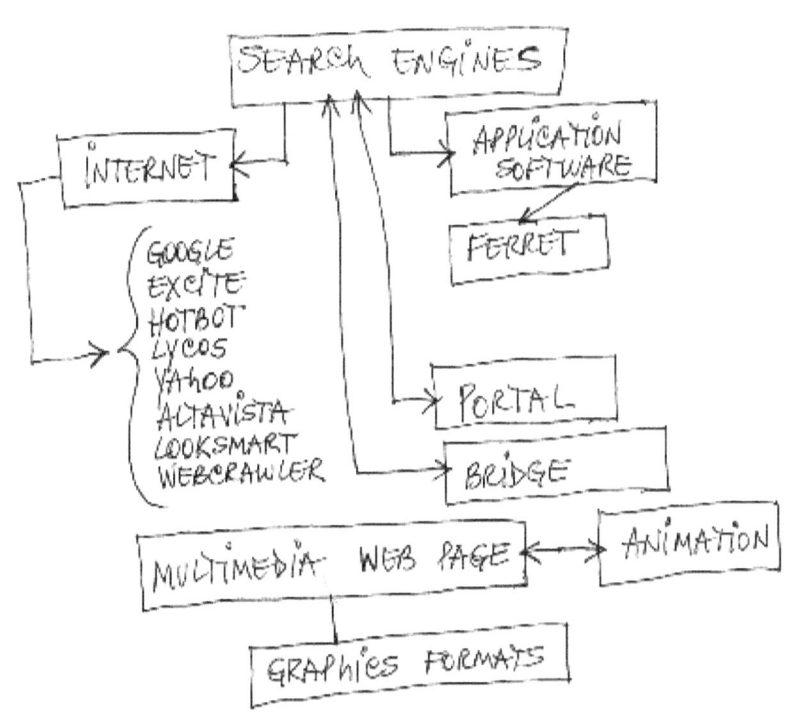

BMP. BIT MAP
GIF. GRAPHICS INTERCHANGE FORMAT
JPEG. JOINT PHOTOGRAPHIC EXPERTS
                          GROUP.
PCX. PC PAINTBRUSH
PNG. PORTABLE NETWORK GRAPHICS
TIFF. TAGGED IMAGE FILE FORMAT

GETTING THE HIDDEN BATTERY REPORT IN
WINDOWS 7, 8, and 10. __

The active Status of the Battery on the User
Computer can be obtained using the CMD
<u>Command Line Utility</u> built into Windows.

Type CMD in the Startup Window in Windows,
then make a <u>shortcut</u> of the CMD desktop App; right
click on it and select" <u>Run as Administrator"</u> then
type: powercfg /batteryreport and press
<Enter> a file on the Hard Drive, in

C:\windows\system 32\batteryreport.html is
created.

Go to C:\windows\system 32 folder and look for
the file; *battery_report* that was just created on the C
Drive to Print it or View it.

```
Administration Command Prompt                                    —   □   ×
Microsoft Windows [Version 10.0.16299.431]
(c) 2017 Microsoft Corporation. All rights reserved.

C:\WINDOWS\system32>powercfg/batteryreport
Battery life report saved to file path C:\WINDOWS\system32\battery-
report.html.

C:\WINDOWS\system32>_
```

BackgroundTransferHost	9/29/2017 6:4
BamSettingsClient.dll	9/29/2017 6:4
BarcodeProvisioningPlugin.dll	9/29/2017 6:4
basecsp.dll	3/29/2018 9:4
basesrv.dll	9/29/2017 6:4
batmeter.dll	1/27/2018 4:2
battery-report	9/23/2018 8:4
bcastdvr	2/9/2018 9:4
bcastdvr.proxy.dll	9/29/2017 6:4
BcastDVRBroker.dll	9/29/2017 6:4
BcastDVRClient.dll	9/29/2017 6:4
BcastDVRCommon.dll	9/29/2017 6:4

The battery report created is an html file. Doubleclick on it to open it in the Web Browser.

DR ALFONSO J. KINGLOW

ABOUT THE AUTHOR
DR ALFONSO J. KINGLOW PHD

Professor Alfonso J. Kinglow have been teaching Computers, Networking and Science and Technology for many years. As an Adjunct Faculty member of NMSU New Mexico State University, in Las Cruces he started Computer classes for Seniors and beginners for several years at Munson Senior Center, in Las Cruces, and presently at

Shadow Mountain Senior Center, in Phoenix, Arizona where he serves as a Volunteer. His classes are very successful and are always full. This Book shares Professor Kinglow vision in bringing modern Technology to all Users as well as Seniors and Beginners trying to keep up with Technology, in a very basic and comprehensive format that is easy to understand. It contains Graphic figures in a box format that makes it easy to convey the information, not just in text mode. The book contains all the built-in System Tools, and some hidden System and User Tools to empower the users to better understand their Computer Hardware and Software, and to be able to Maintain and Setup their own Computers and Security. With information on the new Wi-Fi Standard and other updated System information.

Professor Kinglow received his PhD and many other Awards and is the author of many technical innovations published by NASA. He received the October 2013 Volunteer Spotlight Award from The City of
Las Cruces, and is featured in "Las Cruces Magazine" published by real View publishing, Las Cruces NM.

Dr. Kinglow have taught overseas at various Universities as a bilingual visiting Professor, and is a Systems Engineer by trade. While working for NASA he received the NASA STS-34 Award for outstanding dedication and Mission Support for the Galileo Mission. Dr.

Kinglow received many Commendations and
Honors from NASA for his support of the Shuttle Missions., and is a member of The Computer Society.

This is not the End.

www.ingramcontent.com/pod-product-compliance
Lightning Source LLC
Chambersburg PA
CBHW030918180526
45163CB00002B/389